Understanding IAS 7
Cash flow statements

Part of the IFRS in the UK series

Understanding IAS 7
Cash flow statements

By PricewaterhouseCoopers LLP's UK Accounting Technical Department
London, November 2003

Published by

145 London Road
Kingston upon Thames
Surrey
KT2 6SR
Tel: +44(0) 870 241 5719
Fax: +44(0) 870 247 1184
E-mail: info@cch.co.uk
Website: www.cch.co.uk

Appendix 1 is reproduced with the permission of the International Accounting Standards Board (IASB)

ISBN 1-84140-411-X

Typeset by Kerrypress Ltd, Luton
Printed and bound in Great Britain by Hendy Banks Colour Print.

Acknowledgement

PricewaterhouseCoopers LLP acknowledges the contributions of the following members of UK Accounting Technical in preparing this book:

Yvonne Dinwoodie
Jyoti Ghosh
Peter Holgate
Barry Johnson
Helen McCann
Barbara Willis

November 2003

Contents

Chapter 1

Executive summary

1.1   The principal requirements for preparing a cash flow statement in accordance with international financial reporting standards are summarised in the following paragraphs.

1.2   IAS 7, 'Cash flow statements', requires the reporting of movements of cash and cash equivalents, classified as arising from three main activities - operating, investing and financing.

1.3   All entities must include a cash flow statement as part of their financial statements. There are no exemptions available from the requirement to prepare a cash flow statement.

1.4   Cash equivalents are defined as *'short-term, highly liquid investments, that are readily convertible to known amounts of cash and which are subject to an insignificant risk of changes in value'*. Short-term is viewed by IAS 7 as equating to investments with an original maturity of three months or less.

1.5   No specific format is prescribed by the standard. It requires the presentation of cash flows under the three main classifications of operating, investing and financing activities. However, it does not set out a sequence to be followed. Instead, it allows cash flows to be reported in the manner most appropriate to the entity.

1.6   Cash flows from operating activities may be reported using the direct (gross) or indirect (net) method. Where the indirect method is used, a reconciliation between the net profit reported in the income statement and the net cash flow from operating activities has to be presented. Analysis of the net cash flow from operating activities using the direct method is encouraged, but is not required.

1.7 Entities with foreign currency transactions or foreign operations should present the reporting currency equivalent of foreign currency cash flows, using the exchange rate ruling at the date of the transaction or an exchange rate that approximates to the actual rate (for example, the average rate for the period).

1.8 Foreign currency movements on cash and cash equivalents should be reported separately in the cash flow statement to allow the reconciliation of the opening and closing balances of cash and cash equivalents.

1.9 Cash flows that result from derivative transactions undertaken to hedge another transaction should be classified under the same activity as cash flows from the transaction that is subject to the hedge.

1.10 Where a parent prepares consolidated financial statements, it should prepare a consolidated cash flow statement as if the group were a single entity, with intra-group cash flows eliminated. The cash flows of entities accounted for on an equity basis should be included only to the extent that they reflect cash movements between those entities and the group. The cash flows of those entities that are accounted for on a proportional consolidation basis should be included in the cash flow statement to the extent of the group's proportional share of those cash flows.

1.11 A note is required that discloses the components of cash and cash equivalents used for the cash flow statement. This should provide a reconciliation between the cash and cash equivalents balance from the cash flow statement to the relevant items on the balance sheet.

1.12 Where a group acquires or disposes of a subsidiary, the amounts of cash and cash equivalents paid or received in respect of the consideration should be reported in the cash flow statement, net of any cash and cash equivalent balances transferred as part of the purchase or sale. IAS 7 also requires disclosure in the notes to the cash flow statement of the full purchase or disposal consideration, detailing any cash and cash equivalents element and the separate disclosure of the amounts of cash and cash equivalents transferred as part of the subsidiary's net assets in relation to the purchase or sale. Additionally, IAS 7 requires the amount of assets and liabilities acquired or disposed of, by each major category, to be disclosed.

1.13   Material non-cash transactions should be disclosed in a note to the cash flow statement.

1.14   Restricted cash balances should be disclosed in a note to the cash flow statement, including a narrative explanation of any restriction.

Chapter 2

Introduction

2.1   The success, growth and survival of every reporting entity depends on its ability to generate or otherwise obtain cash. Cash flow is a concept that everyone understands and with which they can identify. Reported profit is important to users of financial statements, but so too is the cash flow generating potential of an enterprise. What enables an entity to survive is the tangible resource of cash not profit, which is merely one indicator of financial performance. Thus, owners look for dividends, suppliers and lenders expect payments and repayments, employees receive wages for their services, and the tax authorities are legally entitled to tax revenues due.

2.2   In the UK, the original standard FRS 1, 'Cash flow statements', issued in September 1991 required that the cash flow statement should include all the reporting entity's inflows and outflows of cash and cash equivalents. Although the concept of cash was readily understood, it was the definition of cash equivalents that caused the greatest difficulty in practice. The standard classed deposits with more than three months to maturity when acquired as investments, not cash equivalents. Critics argued that their exclusion from cash equivalents failed to capture their substance. Company treasurers normally take a longer view of their cash management function and do not draw a distinction between investments and cash in the way envisaged by the old FRS 1, or if they do they draw a different distinction. As a result, they believed that the three month rule was of little or no relevance to their treasury management operations and of limited use in assessing the true liquidity position of the company. Critics also argued that a narrow definition of cash equivalents was not consistent with the objective of FRS 1, which asserted that the purpose of the cash flow statement was to assist users of the financial statements in their assessment of the reporting entity's liquidity, viability and financial adaptability.

2.3 As a result of the criticism of the original standard, a revised standard was issued in October 1996. The revised FRS 1 dropped cash equivalents and used only cash (cash in hand and at bank, less overdrafts) as the basis of the cash flows reported in the cash flow statement. In addition, a new format for the cash flow statement was introduced with eight standard headings, subsequently increased to nine in November 1997 following the publication of FRS 9, 'Associates and joint ventures'. Furthermore, the revised standard firmly linked the cash flow statement with the profit and loss account and the balance sheet by introducing a reconciliation of cash flows to the movement in net debt as well as to operating profit.

2.4 This meant that the revised FRS 1 moved the UK further away from international practice. Both the international standard, IAS 7, and the US standard, SFAS 95, involve reporting changes in 'cash and cash equivalents' and allocate cash flows into operating, investing and financing activities. As a result, UK listed companies that are required to apply EU-adopted international financial reporting standards in their consolidated financial statements for accounting periods beginning on or after 1 January 2005 (and other UK companies that adopt IFRS voluntarily after that date) will have to revert to a cash flow statement that focuses on the movements in cash and cash equivalents and allocates cash flows under the three headings as mentioned above.

Chapter 3

Objectives and scope of IAS 7

Objectives

3.1   The principal objective of IAS 7, 'Cash flow statements', is to require entities falling within its scope to report their changes in cash and cash equivalents in the period, classifying these as arising from operating, investing or financing activities. The standard was effective for financial statements prepared under IAS from periods beginning on or after 1 January 1994.

3.2   The cash flow reporting required under IAS 7 provides useful information on liquidity, viability and financial adaptability that is additional to that provided by the income statement and balance sheet. A combination of profitability and liquidity data enables users of financial statements to view both sides of the same coin when assessing corporate viability over time (business survival depends on both profits from operations and sound cash management). Reporting historical cash flows also helps management to discharge its stewardship function by showing an entity's past cash flows, solvency and liquidity performance. Although historical cash flows are not necessarily a good indicator of future cash flows, they may nevertheless help users to review the accuracy of their previous predictions and, therefore, act as a base for assessing future cash flow performance and liquidity.

3.3   The standard sets out how cash flows should be classified and reported under operating, investing and financing activities. It does not specify a required sequence for these to be presented in the cash flow statement, instead stating that an entity should report its cash flows in a manner most appropriate to the business. [IAS 7 para 11]. However, in practice, most companies reporting under IAS keep to the order of operating, investing and financing activities.

Scope

3.4 IAS 7 requires all entities to prepare a cash flow statement as an integral part of their financial statements for each period for which financial statements are presented. [IAS 7 para 1]. There are no exemptions from the preparation of a cash flow statement under IAS 7. This is in stark contrast to current practice in the UK where there are a number of exemptions available under FRS 1. Therefore, entities currently exempt from preparing a cash flow statement under UK GAAP, for example small companies/groups or 90 per cent owned subsidiary undertakings included in their parent's consolidated financial statements, would be required to prepare a cash flow statement under IAS.

Chapter 4

Preparation of cash flow statements

4.1   A cash flow statement should focus on identifying the cash effects of transactions with parties that are external to the reporting entity and their impact on its cash position. Only those transactions that involve a cash flow should be reported in the cash flow statement. Cash flows are defined as *'inflows and outflows of cash and cash equivalents'*. [IAS 7 para 6].

Definition of cash and cash equivalents

4.2   As the cash flow statement reflects movements in cash and cash equivalents, the definition of these are central to its proper preparation. The definitions of cash and cash equivalents include any such items that are denominated in foreign currencies.

4.3   Consistent with common usage, the definition of cash includes not only cash in hand, but also demand deposits. [IAS 7 para 6]. No guidance is given in IAS 7 for the definition of a demand deposit. However, these are generally accepted to be deposits with financial institutions which are repayable on demand, and available within 24 hours, or one working day, without penalty. Demand deposits, therefore, will include accounts where additional funds may be deposited at any time and funds withdrawn at any time without prior notice, for example, a bank current account.

4.4   Additionally, bank overdrafts that are repayable on demand and that are integral to the company's cash management can be included as a component of cash and cash equivalents. [IAS 7 para 8]. (See further para 4.20.)

4.5 *Cash equivalents*, are defined as:

"Short-term, highly liquid investments that are readily convertible to known amounts of cash and which are subject to an insignificant risk of changes in value."

[IAS 7 para 6].

4.6 In order to meet the definition of cash equivalents in IAS 7, an investment will normally have to have a *'short maturity'*. The standard goes on to suggest that a short maturity period would be a period of three months or less from the date of acquisition of the investment. [IAS 7 para 7]. (See further para 4.13.) The use of a short maturity period when considering investments as cash equivalents incorporates the fact that the investments should be so near to cash that there is insignificant risk of changes in value.

4.7 Those investments that may potentially be classified as cash equivalents are not restricted to investments with financial institutions, such as banks. Provided the definitions of cash equivalents are met, then other types of investments, for example, short-term gilts, certificates of deposits, money market instruments and short-term corporate bonds, may also be classified as cash equivalents under IAS 7. [IAS 7 para 7].

4.8 Furthermore, for a security to be a cash equivalent, it must not only be readily convertible and have a short maturity, it should also be considered as a cash equivalent by the entity that holds it and not be held as an investment or for any other purpose. [IAS 7 para 9]. For the entity to treat a security as a cash equivalent, that security must be regarded as cash or be part of the cash equivalent policy and so considered as a means of settling the entity's liabilities. It follows that not all short-term investments that meet the definition of cash equivalents are required to be treated as such. For example, banking companies might decide to treat all short-term highly liquid investments, except those purchased for its trading account, as cash equivalents, while an investing company may decide that all its short-term highly liquid investments should be treated as investments rather than cash equivalents. Therefore, IAS 7 requires an entity to disclose the policy that it adopts in determining the composition of its cash equivalents. [IAS 7 para 46]. Any change in that policy is regarded as a change in accounting policy and should be accounted for in accordance with IAS 8. [IAS 7 para 47].

4.9 One impact of the definition of cash and cash equivalents is that monies transferred between those deposits or investments that qualify as cash and cash equivalents do not result in cash inflows and outflows, but are merely movements within the overall cash and cash equivalents balance. For instance, a transfer from a demand deposit account to reduce the company's overdraft would not be reflected in cash flows as it is an intra-cash and cash equivalents movement. However, all charges and credits on accounts or investments qualifying as cash and cash equivalents, such as bank interest, bank fees, deposits or withdrawals other than movements wholly within them, represent cash inflows and outflows of the reporting entity

4.10 The complexity of the definition of cash equivalents, which is central to cash flow reporting under IAS 7, may cause difficulties in practice. Therefore, it is necessary to consider the various terms used in the definition further.

Meaning of 'readily convertible'

4.11 The term 'readily convertible' implies that the investment would be convertible into cash without notice, that is, not subject to any time restriction. Therefore, monies deposited in a bank account for an unspecified period, but which can only be withdrawn by giving notice, would not strictly fall to be treated as cash equivalents under the definition. Nevertheless, such funds can always be withdrawn by paying a penalty. However, if the penalty incurred on withdrawal is not significant enough to cause any appreciable change in the capital amount withdrawn and the notice period for withdrawal by incurring a penalty payment is short, for example, seven days, the exclusion of such a deposit from cash equivalents may give a nonsensical result, as it is nearer to cash than a deposit treated as a cash equivalent because it has a maturity period of less than three months. Clearly, that is not the intended effect of the definition and the phrase 'readily convertible' should generally be interpreted as 'convertible without an undue period of notice and without the incidence of a significant penalty on withdrawal'. This means that the facts of each circumstance should take into account the way in which such deposits are viewed and used. Cash deposited with up to, say, one month's notice and which could be withdrawn without significant penalty could, therefore, fall within cash equivalents without offending the spirit of the definition.

Maturity threshold

4.12 Companies normally use a range of instruments for cash management, investing and financing purposes. Such instruments may include bank borrowings, gilts, money market instruments, commercial paper, Euronotes, etc. Although many of these instruments are readily convertible and can be held for the short-term, only those highly liquid instruments that are subject to insignificant risk of changes in value comprise cash equivalents.

4.13 Clarification of this point is given in IAS 7, which indicates that an investment with a short maturity from the date of acquisition will generally qualify as a cash equivalent, provided it is used for cash management purposes. The standard goes on to suggest that a short maturity period would be a three month period. [IAS 7 para 7]. Although any limit on maturity is somewhat arbitrary, it incorporates the fact that investments that are so near cash will have insignificant risk that they will change in value in response to risks such as interest rate risks and market capital value risks.

4.14 The three month maturity period commences from the time the investment was acquired. [IAS 7 para 7]. Any investment, such as a gilt or a certificate of deposit, purchased with a maturity period of more than three months will not be a cash equivalent as the maturity of these instruments exposes them to fluctuations in capital value. Additionally, they will not become a cash equivalent when their remaining maturity period, measured from a subsequent balance sheet date, becomes three months or less, as the maturity period is measured from the date of acquisition.

Example

An entity purchased a bond on 1 October 20X2. The bond's maturity date is 28 February 20X3 and entity's financial year end is 31 December.

The bond should not be classified as a cash equivalent. At the date of acquisition, the maturity of the bond is five months. This does not comply with the short maturity of three months or less from the date of acquisition, suggested in IAS 7. The fact that the bond matures less than three months from the balance sheet date will not result in its classification as a cash equivalent at that point. The interpretation of a short maturity period is a maturity of three months from the *date of acquisition* not from the balance sheet date.

4.15 The standard specifically excludes equity investments from cash equivalents, unless they are cash equivalents in substance. This is due to the high risk of changes in capital value, despite the fact that they can be readily marketable and convertible into cash. The example given in the standard where an investment in shares could be classified as a cash equivalent is where preference shares have been purchased with a set redemption date and a short maturity period.

4.16 Where the counterparty to any short term investment demonstrates that it is experiencing financial problems there may be doubt over their ability to fulfil the requirements of the agreement. In such circumstances the entity should not classify this investment as a cash equivalent as there is a risk that the cash will not be readily convertible or that the maturity date will not be met.

4.17 Prior to its revision in 1996, the original FRS 1 required entities to report movements in cash and cash equivalents in a manner similar to those in IAS 7. Experience of this standard in the UK indicated that many companies believed the definition of cash equivalents was unnecessarily restrictive. For example, one of the objectives of a company's cash management programme is often to earn interest on temporarily idle funds rather than to put capital at risk in the hope of benefiting from capital value changes. Such funds may be placed in a medium-term

13

deposit account to be drawn down for later use. These deposits do not carry any significant risks of changes in value, however, because they mature more than three months from the deposit date, they are excluded from the definition of cash equivalents. Companies normally take a longer view of their cash management function and do not draw a distinction between investments and cash in the way envisaged. As a result, companies believed that the three month maturity rule had the effect of excluding instruments integral to their treasury management operation and regarded it as being of limited use in assessing the true liquidity position of the company.

4.18   In practice, companies dealt with this problem in a variety of ways. Generally companies tended to follow the strict definition of cash and cash equivalents in preparing their cash flow statements, but adapted the format and/or gave additional information that reflect the way in which they managed their cash flows.

4.19   IAS 7 is not necessarily as prescriptive in its enforcement of the three month rule. Under FRS 1 in the UK, the three month maturity was included in the cash and cash equivalents' definition whilst under IAS 7 it is a suggested maturity period, although it is generally applied in practice. IAS 7 also places more emphasis on the purpose of the investment when determining cash equivalents. Therefore, this problem may not be as pronounced under IAS 7 as it was under FRS 1, however, the IAS 7 definition still includes a requirement for the cash equivalent to be so 'near cash' as to be equivalent to cash, so problems will potentially still arise.

Treatment of borrowings

4.20   IAS 7 states that bank borrowings are normally classified as financing activities. However, the standard notes that in certain circumstances, bank overdrafts that are repayable on demand are used in the cash management of the company. Where this is the case, IAS 7 states that the bank overdraft should be included as a component of cash and cash equivalents. [IAS 7 para 8].

4.21 In the UK, under FRS 1, bank overdrafts are required to be deducted from cash for the cash flow statement because they are generally regarded as negative cash balances and repayable on demand. IAS 7, however, states that bank overdrafts are generally considered to be financing activities, but in some countries overdrafts that are repayable on demand are an integral part of an entity's cash management. A characteristic of such banking arrangements is that the bank balance fluctuates from being positive to overdrawn. In such situations overdrafts are included as a component of cash and cash equivalents, which is current practice in the UK as stated above.

4.22 An example of a company including bank overdrafts in cash and cash equivalents is given in Table 1. An example of a company that excludes bank overdrafts from cash and cash equivalents is given in Table 2.

Table 1 – Bank overdrafts included in cash and cash equivalents

Jardine Matheson Holdings Limited – Annual Report – 31 December 2002

35 Notes to Consolidated Cash Flow Statement (extract)

	2002	2001
(i) Analysis of balances of cash and cash equivalents	US$m	US$m
Bank balances and other liquid funds *(refer note 22)*	1,273	959
Bank overdrafts *(refer note 24)*	(28)	(50)
	1,245	909

Principal Accounting Policies (extract)

Cash and Cash Equivalents

For the purposes of the cash flow statement, cash and cash equivalents comprise deposits with banks and financial institutions, bank and cash balances, and liquid investments, net of bank overdrafts. In the balance sheet, bank overdrafts are included in borrowings in current liabilities.

Table 2 – Bank overdrafts excluded from cash and cash equivalents

Kuehne & Nagel International AG – Annual Report – 31 December 2002

Notes to the Consolidated Financial Statements (extract)

9 Cash and cash equivalents

Cash and cash equivalents comprise of cash at bank and in hand and short term deposits with an original maturity of three months or less. For the purpose of the consolidated cash flow statement, cash and cash equivalents consist as defined above.

31 Cash and cash equivalents CHF '000	31/12/2002	31/12/2001
Cash on hand	1,744	1,999
Current and deposit accounts with banks (incl. postal accounts)	775,075₁	244,611
	776,819	246,610

₁ of which CHF 373 million is deposited in a bank account as collateral for a US$ bank overdraft

---

4.23   Therefore, except for bank overdrafts, cash flows from all forms of borrowings (including short-term borrowings of three months or less) are reported gross within financing activities. However, in some situations, IAS 7 permits movements in short-term borrowings to be reported net within financing activities. This would apply where for items where the turnover is quick, the amounts large and the maturities short. [IAS 22 para 22(b)]. (See further para 5.15.)

Sales and purchases of cash and cash equivalents

4.24   Sales and purchases of instruments that are treated as cash equivalents do not result in cash inflows and outflows, but are merely movements within the overall cash and cash equivalents balance. [IAS 7 para 9]. For example, the investment of excess cash in hand into a gilt with short maturity would not be reflected as a movement within cash and cash equivalents.

Chapter 5

Format of cash flow statements

5.1   To achieve the objective of providing information to help investors, creditors and others in making assessments about the liquidity, viability and financial adaptability of an entity, the standard requires cash flows to be classified and reported according to the activity which gave rise to them. There are three standard activities:

- Operating activities.
- Investing activities.
- Financing activities.

[IAS 7 para 10].

5.2   IAS 7 does not specify a layout for the cash flow statement, instead entities should report their cash flows in the manner deemed most appropriate to their business. [IAS 7 para 11]. However, in practice, most companies reporting under IAS keep to the order of operating, investing and financing activities. The elements of cash receipts and payments should be listed under each of the above three standard headings, which together make up the movement of cash and cash equivalents for the period. This net movement is normally added to the balance of cash and cash equivalents that is brought forward at the beginning of the period to give the balance at the end of the period as shown in the illustrative examples in IAS 7.

5.3   Additionally, the effect of exchange rate changes on cash and cash equivalents held or due in foreign currency should be presented on the face of the cash flow statement, albeit separately from cash flows from operating, investing and financing activities, in order to reconcile the cash and cash equivalents at the beginning and end of the period, notwithstanding the fact that such unrealised gains or losses are not cash flows (see also para 7.2). [IAS 7 para 28].

Classification of cash flows

5.4   As stated above, entities must classify cash flows under three standard headings in a manner deemed most appropriate to their business [IAS 7 para 11]. The classification of cash flows by activity provides useful analysis about the relative importance of each of these activities and the inter-relationship between them. It should also provide useful information for comparison purposes across reporting entities.

5.5   The standard provides guidance for classifying cash flows which allows a reasonable amount of discretion. A definition is provided for the activities presented under the three standard activities to assist in classification. Additionally, the standard then discusses and gives examples of the cash flows that would be *expected* to be classified under these headings. This is considered further in paragraphs 6.1 onwards.

5.6   The business carried on by the entity will determine the classification of cash flows, for example, dividends received by a venture capital company are likely to be operating activities as its business is to receive a return on investments, whilst a manufacturing company would classify such dividends received under investing activities.

5.7   A single transaction entered into by an entity may result in a number of cash flows that could be classified differently. These should be split out and presented under their respective headings according to their nature, for example, payments in relation to a finance lease should be split into their component parts of capital repayment (classified as financing activity) and interest paid (generally classified as an operating activity - see para 6.32).

Additional classification

5.8   The individual examples of cash inflows and outflows given for each of the standard headings in IAS 7 should not be regarded as depicting a rigid set of classification rules or a benchmark for minimum disclosure. The examples under each heading merely refer to those items that would normally fall to be included under that heading. Within each standard classification there will be a number of different categories of cash receipts and payments. There is also nothing in the standard to suggest that an entity cannot sub-divide further the elements of cash receipts and payments to give a full description of the activities of the business. For example, proceeds from the issue of debentures may be shown separately from the proceeds of other long-term borrowings. The sub-division can also be extended to material cash flows. In fact, where there is a material cash flow for any constituent element described above, the standard requires that 'major classes' of gross receipts and payments should be disclosed separately *on the face of the cash flow statement.* [IAS 7 paras 18, 21]. For example, cash receipts from dividends received may be further sub-divided between dividends received from associated companies, where these are considered to be material, and other dividends received.

5.9   Whatever level of detail is disclosed, it must be sufficient and relevant so that the user is able to understand the relationship between the entity's different activities and the way in which they generate and expend cash. On the other hand, too much information can cloud or obscure key issues, clutter the face of the cash flow statement and make it difficult to understand. The problem is one of striking a balance. There is no definitive solution to this problem, because so much depends on the reporting entity's circumstances and the specific needs and expertise of users.

5.10   Clearly, the standard does not attempt to provide an exhaustive list for classifying different types of cash flows. Inevitably, some items will call for judgement when clarifying their classification. Decisions should be made according to the circumstances of the individual reporting entity and the transaction's substance. Since the transaction's substance also determines the way in which it is normally reported in the income statement and the balance sheet, it follows that there should be consistency of treatment in the cash flow statement and in the other primary statements. Therefore, cash outflows relating to development expenditure capitalised in the balance sheet would fall to be shown under investing activities in the cash flow statement. Another example is the receipt of a government grant. To the extent that the grant is made as a contribution towards fixed assets, the substance argument would require the cash receipt to be classified as an investing activity, irrespective of its treatment in the balance sheet. Similarly grants given as a contribution towards revenue expenditure should be classified as cash flows from operating activities to match their treatment in the income statement.

5.11 Once cash flows have been classified in relation to a specific activity, this classification should be applied consistently.

Gross or net cash flows

5.12 As noted above in paragraph 5.8, IAS 7 generally requires that major classes of receipts and payments should be reported gross in the cash flow statement. Gross cash flows give users more detailed information of the effects of the activities of the business on the cash flows and, therefore, provide more relevant information than net cash flows. There are, however, certain situations where the standard specifically permits the reporting of net cash flows.

5.13 The reporting of gross cash flows does not apply to operating activities where the indirect method is followed (see para 6.9). [IAS 7 para 18].

5.14 Cash receipts and payments on behalf of customers, where these reflect the activities of the customer, can be netted against each other. [IAS para 22(a)]. For instance, where an entity is acting as a disclosed agent on behalf of its customers, cash flows should only reflect the commission received by the agent. The standard gives further examples as follows:

- The acceptance and repayment of demand deposits of a bank.
- Funds held for customers by an investment enterprise.

- Rents collected on behalf of, and paid over to, the owners of properties.

[IAS 7 para 23].

5.15 Cash receipts and payments may also be reported net for items where the turnover is quick, the amounts large and the maturities short. [IAS 22 para 22(b)]. IAS 7 gives the following examples of where this can arise:

- Advances and repayments of credit card principal amounts.
- The purchase and sale of investments.
- Other short-term borrowings (for example, three months or less).

[IAS 7 para 23].

5.16 For example, an entity may periodically raise funding by issuing commercial paper, say, in the form of unsecured promissory notes with fixed maturity of between seven and ninety days. This may result in numerous issues and redemptions during the year, which are backed by committed bank facilities. The cash flows in relation to these short-term loans will be classified as cash flows arising from financing activities and may be reported on a net basis. In this case, the disclosure of the gross cash receipts and payments will not provide additional information necessary to understand the entity's financing activity. A better understanding of the entity's financing activities is achieved where these potentially large inflows and outflows, for what may in substance be a continuing source of finance, are reported on a net basis.

5.17 IAS 7 permits an entity to report the purchases and sales of investments on a net basis under investing. However, this is only where the conditions in paragraph 22(b) of IAS 7 are met, that is, where the turnover is quick, the amounts large and the maturities short. In practice, the reporting of cash flows on a net basis for investments will usually only arise in a bank or similar financial institution. Therefore, for a non-bank (or similar) entity the purchases and sales of investments should normally be shown gross. An exception may be where amounts are placed on deposit and continually rolled-over.

5.18 The following cash flows can be reported net for financial institutions:

• Cash receipts and payments for the acceptance and repayment of deposits with a fixed maturity date.
• The placement of deposits with and withdrawal of deposits from other financial institutions.
• Cash advances and loans made to customers and the repayment of those advances and loans.

[IAS 7 para 24].

The above net presentation is appropriate in the consolidated cash flow statement of a group that includes a subsidiary undertaking that is a financial institution, even though gross cash flows would be reported for the group's other operations.

Chapter 6

Classification of cash flows by standard headings

Cash flow from operating activities

6.1 IAS 7 defines operating activities as *"the principal revenue-producing activities of the enterprise and other activities that are not investing or financing activities"*. [IAS 7 para 6]. Therefore, by definition, cash flows from operating activities represent the cash effects of transactions and other events relating to the principal revenue-producing activities of the entity. Generally, cash flows from operating activities will represent the movements in cash and cash equivalents resulting from the operations shown in the income statement in arriving at net profit or loss. [IAS 7 para 14]. The separate disclosure of operating activity cash flows allows the user of the financial statements to assess the extent to which the operating activities generate cash flows to maintain the operating capability of the entity and support the cash flows for financing and investing activities.

6.2 Some transactions giving rise to amounts included in net profit or loss will not be classified as operating cash flows, for example, the cash flow relating to a gain on sale of a fixed asset will be reported under investing activities (see para 6.16).

6.3 IAS 7 gives the following examples of cash flows that are expected to be classified as operating activities:

• Receipts from the sale of goods and the rendering of services.
• Receipts from royalties, fees, commissions and other revenue.

- Payments to suppliers for goods and services.
- Payments to and on behalf of employees.
- For an insurance entity, receipts and payments for premiums and claims, annuities and other policy benefits.
- Payments and refunds of income taxes (unless they can be specifically identified as financing or investing).
- Receipts and payments from contracts held for dealing or trading purposes.

[IAS 7 para 14].

6.4   Where an entity deals or trades in securities, this is equivalent to inventory in a retail company and, therefore, this activity will fall to be treated as operating activities. In a similar vein, financial institutions will classify cash flows in relation to advances of loans to customers within operating activities. [IAS 7 para 15].

6.5   Operating cash flows may be reported using either the direct method (see para 35.70) or the indirect method (see para 6.6). [IAS 7 para 18].

Direct method

6.6   The direct method reports the major classes of *gross* operating cash receipts (for example, cash collected from customers) and gross operating cash payments (for example, cash paid to suppliers and employees). These gross operating cash flows are aggregated to produce the net operating cash flow of the entity. This presentation is consistent with that of investing and financing activities. The following is an extract from the cash flow statement of an entity that presents its cash flows from operating activities using the direct method:

Cash flows from operating activities	
Cash receipts from customers	x
Cash paid to suppliers and employees	(x)
Cash generated from operations	x
Interest paid	(x)
Income taxes paid	(x)
Net cash from operating activities	x

6.7 There are essentially two ways in which gross operating cash receipts and payments may be derived under the direct method. They may be captured directly from a separate cash-based accounting system that records amounts paid or received in any transaction. Alternatively, they may also be determined indirectly by adjusting operating profit and loss account items for non-cash items, changes in working capital and other items that relate to investing and financing cash flows. [IAS 7 para 19]. For example, cash collected from customers may be derived indirectly by adjusting sales for the changes in amounts receivable from customers during the period. Similarly, cash paid to suppliers for goods used in manufacture or resale may be determined indirectly by adjusting cost of sales for changes in inventory and amounts due to suppliers during the period.

6.8 The standard encourages, but does not require, reporting entities to use the direct method. [IAS 7 para 19]. This is because the direct method produces a cash flow statement in its purest form with new information that is not otherwise available from the profit and loss account and the balance sheet. However, in spite of its theoretical soundness, the direct method could impose excessive implementation costs. Many companies may not collect information that will allow them to determine gross cash receipts and payments directly from the accounting system. Although the information under the direct method could be obtained under the alternative method discussed above by making appropriate adjustments, it is considered that the more detailed the categories of operating cash receipts and payments to be reported, the more complex will be the procedure for determining them. Therefore, this approach may require significant incremental costs over those required under the indirect method (see below), because it would involve the sub-categorisation of debtors and creditors. Very few companies have the need to derive cash receipts and payments on operating cash flow in this way. For the reasons stated above, the direct method has not been popular and, the indirect method, described below, is more commonly used.

Indirect method

6.9   Under the indirect method, the same total cash flows from operating activities as under the direct method are ultimately reported, except that the figure is produced by adjusting the net profit or loss to remove the effects of non-cash items (such as depreciation and provisions), changes in working capital (such as accruals and prepayments and changes in receivables and payables in the period) and items that relate to investing and financing activities. [IAS 7 para 20]. This will reconcile the net profit or loss to the cash flow from operating activities. The reconciliation may be presented in a note or on the face of the cash flow statement. Specific items included in cash flows from operating activities such as interest and tax paid must, however, be presented on the face of the cash flow statement. [IAS 7 paras 32 and 35].

6.10   The following is an extract from the cash flow statement of an entity that presents its cash flows from operating activities using the indirect method:

Cash flows from operating activities	
Net profit before taxation	x
Adjustments for:	
Depreciation	x
Foreign exchange loss	x
Investment income	(x)
Interest expense	x

Operating profit before working capital changes	x
Increase in trade and other receivables	(x)
Decrease in inventories	x
Decrease in trade payables	(x)
Cash generated from operations	x
Interest paid	(x)
Income taxes paid	(x)
Net cash from operating activities	x

6.11 The standard allows an alternative presentation under the indirect method to that in paragraph 6.8. This shows the revenues and expenses disclosed in the income statement and the adjustments for changes in working capital and non-cash movements in the period to give the cash flows. [IAS 7 para 20]. An example is given in Appendix A to IAS 7, but this type of presentation is rarely used in practice.

6.12 IAS 7 describes the indirect method as a method *". . . whereby net profit or loss is adjusted for the effects of transactions of a non-cash nature, any deferrals or accruals of past or future operating cash receipts or payments, and items of income or expense associated with investing or financing cash flows"*. [IAS 7 para 18(b)]. Net profit or loss under international standards is generally taken to mean the same as profit or loss for the period under UK GAAP, that is profit after tax and minority interests. However, the example in the appendix to the standard begins the reconciliation, not with net profit for the period, but with 'net profit before taxation and extraordinary items' (extraordinary items are allowed under IAS 8, but they are expected to be prohibited in due course). This ambiguity in the standard is rather unsatisfactory.

6.13 In general, the reconciliation of net profit or loss to net cash flows from operating activities will disclose movements in inventory, debtors and creditors related to operating activities, other non-cash items (for example, depreciation, provisions, gain or loss on sale of assets, share of profits of associated companies and minority interest) and other items, such as interest and taxation, which are required to be shown separately.

For the reconciliation to be properly carried out, it will be necessary to analyse the movements in opening and closing debtors and creditors in order to eliminate those movements that relate to items reported in financing or investing activities. For example, a company may purchase a fixed asset prior to the year end on credit. In this situation, the closing creditors balance would need to be adjusted to eliminate the amount owing for the fixed asset purchase before working out the balance sheet movements for operating creditors.

6.14 It follows that movements in working capital would not necessarily be the same as the difference between the opening and the closing balance sheet amounts. This is because the balance sheet movements in inventory, debtors, and creditors may be affected by such items as acquisitions and disposals of subsidiaries during the year (see para 8.10), exchange differences on working capital of foreign subsidiaries (see para 9.18) and other non-cash adjustments for opening and closing accruals for non-operating items.

6.15 A question arises as to whether the eliminated items within each balance sheet movement of working capital need to be reported separately so that the overall movement between the opening and closing balance sheet amounts is readily understandable. For example, a company could identify the total balance sheet movement in creditors and then separately itemise the operating element and the other movements. The standard is silent on this point and in practice, this is rarely done; only the operating movement is reported. Whether shareholders, investors and other users of financial statements are really interested in this degree of detail is debatable as it serves no more than a mere arithmetical check.

Cash flow from investing activities

6.16 IAS 7 defines investing activities as *"the acquisition and disposal of long-term assets and other investments not included in cash equivalents"*. [IAS 7 para 6]. Cash flows from investing activities, therefore, generally include the cash effects of transactions relating to the acquisition and disposal of any fixed asset or current asset investment (other than those regarded as cash equivalents). This includes any cash flows relating to the acquisition or disposal of equity interests in other entities (including subsidiaries, associates and joint ventures) or business units. The disclosure of cash flows from investing activities provides users with information on the extent of expenditure which has been incurred in order to generate the future cash flows and profits of the business.

6.17 IAS 7 gives the following examples of cash flows expected to be classified as investing activities:

- Payments to acquire long-term assets (including property, plant and equipment, intangibles and payments relating to capitalised development costs and self-constructed property, plant and equipment).
- Receipts from sales of long-term assets.
- Payments to acquire equity or debt instruments of other entities and interests in joint ventures (other than payments for those instruments considered to be cash equivalents or those held for dealing or trading purposes). See further paragraph 8.8 onwards for required disclosures in relation to the purchase of equity interests in subsidiaries.
- Receipts from the sale of equity or debt instruments of other entities and interests in joint ventures (other than payments for those instruments considered to be cash equivalents or those held for dealing or trading purposes). See further paragraph 8.8 onwards for required disclosures in relation to the disposal of equity interests in subsidiaries.
- Advances and loans made to other parties (other than those made by a financial institution).
- Receipts from the repayment of advances and loans made to other parties (other than those received by a financial institution).
- Payments for futures, forwards, options and swaps, except when the contracts are held for dealing or trading purposes, or the payments are classified as financing activities.

- Receipts for futures, forwards, options and swaps, except when the contracts are held for dealing or trading purposes, or the receipts are classified as financing activities.

[IAS 7 para 16].

6.18 Where any of the items in the examples given are held for dealing or trading purposes then their cash flows will be reported under operating activities rather than investing (see para 6.4). In addition, cash flows in relation to derivatives, such as futures, that are used in respect of the financing activities of the entity will be classified under financing activities. When a derivative contract is accounted for as a hedge of an identifiable position, the cash flows in relation to that contract should be classified in the same manner as the cash flows of the position being hedged (see para 9.21).

6.19 The cash payments disclosed for the acquisition of long-term assets will include any capitalised development costs and costs incurred in the construction of an asset by the entity for its own use. Any interest capitalised in relation to a borrowing for capital expenditure will be presented in the total interest balance presented on the cash flow statement. (see para 6.29).

6.20 The amount paid in respect of fixed assets during the year may not be the same as the amount of additions shown in the fixed asset note. The difference may be due to a number of reasons. For example, fixed assets may be purchased on credit, in which case the amounts for additions shown in the fixed asset note would need to be adjusted for the outstanding credit to arrive at the cash paid. Furthermore, the change in fixed asset creditors should be eliminated from the total change in creditors, to arrive at the movement in operating creditors, a figure needed for the reconciliation of net profit to net cash flow where the indirect method is used to report cash flows from operating activities (see para 6.13). In addition, where interest has been capitalised during the period and included within fixed assets, the amount so capitalised would need to be deducted to arrive at the correct amount of cash paid for the acquisition or construction of a fixed asset. The amount of capitalised interest that has been paid during the period should be included in the total of interest paid during the period and separately disclosed (see para 6.29). Another example is where fixed assets have been acquired in foreign currencies. In this situation, the sterling equivalent of the foreign currency amount paid in cash that is reported in the cash flow statement is not necessarily the same as the sterling equivalent of the cost recorded at the date of the transaction and included in the balance sheet, because of changes in exchange rates in any period of credit.

6.21 A further example arises where assets have been acquired under finance leases. Most companies do not show assets acquired under finance leases separately, but include them in the total additions figure in their fixed assets movements note. Since assets acquired under finance leases do not involve any cash outlay at the inception of the lease, it will be necessary to eliminate the amount in respect of leased assets that is included in the figure for fixed assets additions so that the true cash outflow for fixed assets purchased can be reflected in the cash flow statement. Any finance lease rental payments should be separated out into their separate components for capital and interest payments. The cash payment in relation to the capital element should be classified under financing activities. [IAS 7 para 17(e)]. The cash payment in relation to the interest element should be treated in the same manner as other interest payable (see further para 6.29).

6.22 A particular problem arises with the treatment of short-term investments, that is, those that fall outside the definition of cash equivalents such that their related cash flows are classified as investing activities. The inclusion of cash flows relating to these instruments as investing activities can distort the total for this category, in particular where these short-term investments are in substance being used by the entity to manage its cash flows, although they do not meet the cash equivalents definition for IAS 7 purposes. For instance, cash that is placed on deposit of more than three months will show as an outflow in the investing section of the cash flow statement. The subsequent maturity of the investment will show as an inflow. If there are a number of transactions in relation to these short-term investments in the period, which is likely where they are being used in such a manner to manage cash flows, this can result in a misleading impression of investing activities as it will reflect large inflows and outflows within investing activities, where in effect the same cash is simply being deposited numerous times throughout the period. However, in some situations it may be possible for an entity to use a net presentation (see para 5.15).

6.23 IAS 7 requires specific treatment and disclosures in relation to the cash flows arising on acquisition or disposal of subsidiaries and other business units. These are further discussed in paragraph 8.8.

6.24 Companies may invest to maintain the entity's existing level of operations (for example, routine replacement of plant and machinery for normal wear and tear) or to expand that level of operations (for example, by investing in new products or services). In practice, there is no clear distinction between these two types of capital expenditure and the criteria used may also differ from company to company. However, some entities may find it useful to make such a distinction. IAS 7, therefore, encourages that the aggregate amount of cash flows that represent increases in operating capacity be disclosed separately from those cash flows that are required to maintain operating capacity. [IAS 7 para 50(c)].

Cash flow from financing activities

6.25 IAS 7 defines financing activities as *"activities that result in changes in the size and composition of the equity capital and borrowings of the enterprise"*. [IAS 7 para 6]. Therefore, cash flows from financing activities generally comprise receipts or payments in relation to the obtaining, servicing and repayment or redemption of debt and equity sources of finance. Separate disclosure of the cash flows from financing activities is useful to the users of the financial statements when determining the manner in which operating and investing activities are being financed.

6.26 The standard gives the following examples of the cash flows expected to be classified as arising from financing activities:

- Receipts from the issue of shares or other equity instruments.
- Payments to acquire or redeem the entity's own shares.
- Receipts from the issue of debentures, loans, notes, bonds, mortgages and other short or long-term borrowings.
- Repayments of amounts borrowed.
- Capital element of finance lease repayments.

[IAS 7 para 17].

Cash flows from derivatives used for financing activities will also be classified under financing activity cash flows (see para 6.17).

6.27   Transaction costs arising on obtaining debt financing, such as fees paid to banks or lawyers on arrangement, are a form of finance cost which is amortised over the life of the instrument and would, therefore, be treated in the same way as any interest payable on that item (see para 6.29). Transaction costs in relation to the issue of equity shares will be classified as financing activity cash flows. No guidance is given in IAS 7 in relation to whether cash flows for equity transactions should be shown gross or net of transaction costs. However, we would recommend that where transaction costs of an equity transaction are material, they should be disclosed separately from the proceeds of the equity instrument under financing activity. This is in keeping with the principle that, in general, cash inflows and outflows should be reported gross. This is particularly relevant where transaction costs relate to the issue of a compound instrument that contains both a liability and an equity element.

6.28   IAS 7 does not deal specifically with the treatment of cash flows on redemption of a deep discounted bond or the premium payable on the redemption of a debt security. This is considered under 'Practical application' (see para 11.4).

Interest and dividend cash flows

6.29   The cash flows arising from dividends and interest receipts and payments should be classified in the cash flow statement under the activity appropriate to their nature. Classification should be on a consistent basis from period to period. Additionally, they are required to be disclosed separately on the face of the cash flow statement. The standard requires disclosure of the total interest paid balance on the cash flow statement, regardless of whether the interest has been expensed or capitalised. [IAS 7 paras 31, 32].

6.30   As with other types of cash flows, IAS 7 does not dictate how the dividends and interest cash flows should be classified for all entities, but rather allows an entity to determine the classification appropriate to its business. It is generally accepted that dividends received and interest paid or received in respect of the cash flows of a financial institution will be classified as operating activities, however, the classification is not so clear cut for other types of companies.

6.31   Therefore, the standard allows the following presentation for interest and dividends received and paid, provided the presentation selected is applied on a consistent basis from period to period:

- Interest and dividends received in operating or investing activities (see Tables 4 and 5).
- Interest and dividends paid in operating or financing activities (see Tables 4 and 6).

6.32   The standard permits companies to show dividends paid in operating activities, because this allows users to determine the ability of an entity to pay dividends out of operating cash flows. [IAS 7 para 34]. Nevertheless, it is likely that most UK companies would categorise interest paid in operating and dividends paid to parent and minority shareholders in financing on the grounds that, although both are payments to providers of capital, interest paid is contractual and has to be paid when due, whereas dividends are discretionary and payments may vary according to the amount legally available for distribution, the cash available and the dividend policy of the entity.

Table 4 – Interest classified as an operating cash flow

Nokia Corporation – Annual Accounts – 31 December 2002

Consolidated cash flow statements, IAS (extract)

Financial year ended Dec. 31	Notes	2002 EURm	2001 EURm	2000 EURm
Cash flow from operating activities				
Net profit		**3 381**	2 200	3 938
Adjustments, total	33	**3 151**	4 132	2 805
Net profit before change in net working capital		**6 532**	6 332	6 743
Change in net working capital	33	**955**	978	-1 377
Cash generated from operations		**7 487**	7 310	5 366
Interest received		**229**	226	255
Interest paid		**-94**	-155	-115
Other financial income and expenses		**139**	99	-454
Income taxes paid		**-1 947**	-933	-1 543
Net cash from operating activities		**5 814**	6 547	3 509

33. Notes to cash flow statement	2002 EURm	2001 EURm	2000 EURm
Adjustments for:			
Depreciation and amortization (Note 9)	**1 311**	1 430	1 009
(Profit)/loss on sale of property, plant and equipment and available-for-sale investments	**-92**	148	-42
Income taxes (Note 11)	**1 484**	1 192	1 784
Share of results of associated companies (Note 32)	**19**	12	16
Minority interest	**52**	83	140
Financial income and expenses (Note 10)	**-156**	-125	-102
Impairment charges	**524**	1 312	-
Other	**9**	80	-
Adjustments, total	**3 151**	4 132	2 805

Change in net working capital			
Decrease (increase) in short-term receivables	**25**	-286	-2 304
Decrease (increase) in inventories	**243**	434	-422
Increase in interest-free short-term liabilities	**687**	830	1 349
Change in net working capital	**955**	978	-1 377
Non-cash investing activities			
Acquisition of:			
Amber Networks	**-**	408	-
Network Alchemy	**-**	-	336
DiscoveryCom	**-**	-	223
Total	**-**	408	559

Table 5 – Interest and dividends received classified as an investing cash flow

Roche Holdings Ltd – Annual Report – 31 December 2002

Consolidated cash flow statement in millions of CHF (extract)	Year ended 31 December	
	2002	2001
Cash flow from investing activities		
Purchase of property, plant and equipment, and intangible assets[14, 15]	(2,139)	(2,140)
Disposal of property, plant and equipment, and intangible assets[14, 15]	283	209
Acquisition of subsidiaries, associated companies and products[33]	(492)	(175)
Divestments of subsidiaries, associated companies and products[33]	217	-
Proceeds from sale of LabCorp shares[12]	1,246	1,420
Interest and dividends received[33]	505	833
Sales (purchases) of marketable securities, net and other investing cash flows	3,918	(3,847)
Total cash flows from (used in) investing activities	3,538	(3,700)

33. Cash flow statement in millions of CHF (extract)

Cash flows from investing activities

Cash flows from investing activities are principally those arising from the Group's investments in property, plant and equipment and intangible assets, and from the acquisition and divestment of subsidiaries, associated companies and businesses. Cash flows connected with the Group's portfolio of marketable securities and other investments are also included as are any interest and dividend payments received in respect of these securities and investments. These cash flows indicate the Group's net reinvestment in its operating assets and the cash flow effects of the changes in Group organisation, as well as the cash generated by the Group's other investments.

Cash flows from marketable securities, including income and capital gains and losses, are shown as a net movement on the Group's portfolio, as these consist of a large number of positions which are not held on a long-term basis. The cash flows from LabCorp transactions (see Note 12) are shown as a separate line in the cash flow statement. The cash flows in respect of Chugai consist of cash payments by Roche to third parties less the cash held by Chugai when acquired.

Acquisitions of subsidiaries, associated companies and products	2002	2001
Chugai[6]	(483)	-
Antisoma[16]	(9)	-
Amira[3]	-	(159)
Other acquisitions	-	(16)
Total	(492)	(175)

Divestments of subsidiaries, associated companies and products	2002	2001
Neupogen[11]	217	-
Other divestments	-	-
Total	217	-

Interest and dividends received	2002	2001
Interest received	428	672
Dividends received	77	161
Total	505	833

Table 6 – Interest and dividends paid classified as a financing cash flow

Roche Holdings Ltd – Annual Report – 31 December 2002

Consolidated cash flow statement in millions of CHF **(extract)**

	Year ended 31 December	
	2002	2001
Cash flows from financing activities		
Proceeds from issue of long-term debt[33]	274	2,110
Repayment of long-term debt[33]	(1,700)	(2,808)
Transactions in own equity instruments[25]	39	706
Increase (decrease) in short-term borrowings	230	867
Interest and dividends paid[33]	(1,794)	(1,900)
Genentech stock repurchases[5]	(1,079)	(67)
Other financing cash flows	89	268
Total cash flows from (used in) financing activities	(3,941)	(824)

33. Cash flow statement in millions of CHF **(extract)**

Cash flows from financing activities

Cash flows from financing activities are primarily the proceeds from issue and repayments of the Group's equity and debt instruments. They also include interest payments and dividend payments on these instruments. Cash flows from short-term financing, including finance leases, are also included. These cash flows indicate the Group's transactions with the providers of its equity and debt financing. Cash flows from short-term borrowings are shown as a net movement, as these consist of a large number of transactions with short maturity.

	2002	2001
Proceeds from issue of long-term debt		
'LYONs V' zero coupon exchangeable US dollar notes due 2021[29]	-	1,689
Long-term bank loans and other borrowings[29]	274	421
Total	274	2,110

Repayment of long-term debt	2002	2001
Repayment of 'Samurai' 1% Japanese yen bonds[29]	(1,258)	-
Repayment of 'Bull Spread' 2.75% US dollar bonds[29]	-	(1,734)
Long-term bank loans and other borrowings[29]	(442)	(1,074)
Total	(1,700)	(2,808)

Interest and dividends paid	2002	2001
Interest paid	(693)	(919)
Dividends paid[25]	(1,101)	(981)
Total	(1,794)	(1,900)

Taxation cash flows

6.33   Cash flows in relation to taxation on income should be classified and separately disclosed under operating activities in the cash flow statement, unless they can be specifically attributed to financing or investing activities. [IAS 7 para 35]. It may be inappropriate and rather misleading to require allocation of tax flows between the three economic activities. A payment of UK corporation tax involves only one cash flow that is arrived at by applying the rate of corporation tax to the entity's total income. The total income is the result of aggregation of taxable income arising from all sources, including chargeable capital gains. The taxation rules under which taxable total income is calculated do not easily lend themselves to subdivision between operating, investing and financing activities. Consequently, any allocation that attempts to segregate the taxation cash flows in this manner may result in the reporting of hypothetical figures in the cash flow statement. For example, the tax effects of investing activities (capital allowances arising on the acquisition of plant and machinery) are set-off against profits arising from operating activities (trading profits). The reporting of a theoretical tax refund due to capital allowances under investing activities will require grossing up the actual tax paid on operating activities. A similar situation arises where the tax effects of trading losses are set-off against capital gains. Clearly, this is not what happens in practice and to present it as such in the cash flow statement would be grossly misleading. Furthermore, as taxation cash flows generally arise from activities in an earlier period, apportioning the taxation cash flows would not necessarily report the taxation cash flows along with the transactions that gave rise to them. Therefore, in general, a UK company would report a single tax cash flow in the cash flow statement under operating activities. This presentation is different from the current practice under FRS 1 where tax cash flows are reported under a separate heading in the cash flow statement, reflecting the fact that tax paid or received is a direct consequence of carrying out all the three activities.

6.34   Where taxation cash flows are disclosed under different activities, the standard requires that the total amount of tax paid in relation to income is disclosed. [IAS 7 para 36]. As discussed above, this disclosure is unlikely to apply to UK companies.

6.35   The standard does not give any guidance on the treatment of VAT or other sales taxes in the cash flow statement. VAT is not a tax on income, therefore, it is not covered by the above paragraphs. Two issues arise in relation to the treatment of VAT in the cash flow statement. First, whether the cash flows should be reported gross or net of VAT. Secondly, how should the net amounts paid to or repaid by Customs & Excise be reported in the cash flow statement.

6.36   The cash flows of an entity include VAT where appropriate and thus strictly speaking the various elements of cash flows from operating, investing and financing activities should include VAT. However, this treatment does not take into account the fact that normally VAT is a short-term timing difference (settled every quarter) as far as the entity's overall cash flows are concerned and the inclusion of VAT in the cash flows may distort the allocation of cash flows to standard headings. In order to avoid this distortion, we believe that cash flows should be shown net of VAT, which is current practice in the UK. For example, payments for fixed assets should be shown net of VAT under investing activities. However, where the VAT falls to be irrecoverable, because the entity carries on an exempt or partially exempt business, or incurs VAT on items that are disallowed (for example, VAT on purchase of motor vehicles), the cash flows should be shown gross of the irrecoverable tax.

6.37 The second issue can be resolved by taking a simple and pragmatic approach. The net movement on the VAT payable to, or receivable from, Customs & Excise would be allocated to cash flows from operating activities unless it is more appropriate to allocate it to another heading. Generally, the majority of the VAT transactions would relate to operating activities, but where a significant proportion of the VAT payments (or receipts) relate to other cash flow headings, such as investing, it may be appropriate to include the net payment (or receipt) under that heading. The effect of including the net movement on the VAT account in operating cash flows means that there will be no need to eliminate the amount of VAT included in opening and closing debtors or creditors when carrying out a reconciliation between net profit and net cash flow from operating activities where the indirect method is used to reporting operating activity cash flows.

6.38 Taxation cash flows excluding those in respect of tax on income and VAT or other sales taxes should be included in the cash flow statement under the same standard headings as the cash flow that gave rise to the taxation cash flows. This presentation is consistent with the manner in which transactions are presented in profit and loss account and balance sheet. For example, employers' national insurance contributions and amounts paid in respect of PAYE to the tax authorities should be included in operating activities. Where the direct method is followed, they will be included in the amounts shown as paid to or on behalf of employees. Similarly, stamp duty incurred in the acquisition of a property would be included in investing activities.

Chapter 7

Reconciliation with balance sheet items

7.1   IAS 7 requires that the components making up the total opening and closing balances of cash and cash equivalents in the cash flow statement should be disclosed and that these should also be reconciled to the appropriate balance sheet line items. [IAS 7 para 45].

7.2   Furthermore, where the reporting entity holds foreign currency cash and cash equivalent balances, then any exchange difference arising on their retranslation at the balance sheet date will have increased or decreased such cash and cash equivalent balances. As such exchange differences do not give rise to any cash flows, they will not be reported as part of the movement in cash and cash equivalents. Consequently, it is necessary to consider such exchange differences in any analysis where movements in cash and cash equivalents are related to opening and closing balances. In fact, IAS 7 requires the effect of exchange rate adjustments on foreign currency cash and cash equivalents (those arising from the retranslation of opening balances of cash and cash equivalents and those arising from translating the cash flows at rates other than the year end rate) to be reported in the cash flow statement to determine the total movement in cash and cash equivalents in the period (see para 5.3). [IAS 7 para 28]. The treatment of exchange differences in the context of the cash flow statement is considered further in paragraph 9.1 onwards.

7.3   In most situations, the reconciliation of opening and closing cash and cash equivalents will be relatively straightforward, because the opening balance of cash and cash equivalents together with the increase or decrease in cash and cash equivalents as shown in the cash flow statement will equate to the closing balance. Where totals for cash and cash equivalents are not readily identifiable, because they relate to separate different balance sheet amounts, sufficient detail should be shown to enable the movements to be understood. This is because cash and cash equivalents per the cash flow statement is not necessarily the same as the single figure on the balance sheet. For example, short-term highly liquid investments and bank overdrafts that are treated as cash equivalents, but are included elsewhere within current assets and current liabilities, must be separately identified for the purposes of the reconciliation.

7.4   An example of disclosure in respect of cash and cash equivalents is as follows:

Cash and cash equivalents

Cash and cash equivalents consist of cash in hand, cash at bank and short-term deposits with financial institutions with original maturity periods of three months or less.

Cash and cash equivalents included in the cash flow statement comprise the following balance sheet amounts:

	20X2 £m	20X1 £m
Cash at bank and in hand	x	x
Short-term bank deposits	x	x
Cash and cash equivalents	x	x

Chapter 8

Consolidated cash flow statements

8.1   The form and content of cash flow statements discussed above applies equally where consolidated financial statements are prepared. Therefore, a parent company of a group that is required to prepare a consolidated balance sheet and a consolidated income statement should prepare a consolidated cash flow statement reflecting the cash flows of the group entity. In preparing consolidated cash flow statements, adjustments should be made to eliminate those cash flows that are internal to the group. Only those cash receipts and payments that flow to and from the group entity as a whole should be included. Many important issues arise in preparing consolidated cash flow statements and these are considered below.

Minority interests

8.2   Where there are minority interests in any subsidiary that is consolidated as part of a group, the treatment of the minority interest in the consolidated cash flow statement should be consistent with the overall approach to the minority interests followed in the preparation of the group financial statements. Companies are required by IAS 27, 'Consolidated financial statements and accounting for investments in subsidiaries', to eliminate intra-group balances and intra-group transactions in the consolidated financial statements. Therefore, they should do the same in preparing a consolidated cash flow statement even where minority interests, which may be substantial, are involved. (For example, where a subsidiary is consolidated because the parent has an ownership interest of say 40 per cent and has the power to appoint or remove the majority of the board of directors, the minority interest could be 60 per cent.) Intra-group transactions should be eliminated because the group, including partly owned subsidiaries, is a single reporting entity for financial reporting purposes. Therefore, in this situation, only cash flows that are external to the group, which includes those with minorities, should be reflected in the cash flow statements. Dividends paid to minority shareholders will generally be classified under financing activities as discussed in paragraph 6.32.

8.3 IAS 32, 'Financial instruments: Disclosure and presentation', requires a subsidiary's financial instruments (including shares) to be shown as liabilities in consolidated financial statements where the parent or any fellow subsidiary undertaking has guaranteed their dividends or redemption, or undertaken to purchase the minority shares if the subsidiary fails to make the expected payments. Where such instruments are classified as liabilities, the dividends paid on those shares should be shown as part of the interest charge in the consolidated income statement. It follows that, in the consolidated cash flow statement, the dividends paid should similarly be shown as interest paid and not as dividends to minorities and, therefore, should be classified consistently with other interest payable (see para 6.29).

Investments accounted for under the equity method

8.4 Where a group has investments in associated undertakings or joint ventures that are included in the consolidation under the equity method, the consolidated cash flow statement should include only the cash flows between the group and those investees, not the cash flows of those entities. [IAS 7 para 37]. This means that the following cash flows should be included:

- Cash flows from sales or purchases between the group and the associate undertakings or joint ventures.
- Cash flows from investments in, and dividends from, the associated undertakings or joint ventures.

8.5 Specifically, the following information should be disclosed separately for equity accounted entities:

- Dividends received from these entities should be classified under operating or investing activities in line with the group's policy for dividends received (see para 6.29).
- Cash flows relating to acquisitions and disposals should be shown under investing activities (see para 6.17).
- Financing cash flows received from or paid to equity accounted entities should be shown under financing.

8.6 The way in which income received from associated undertakings is reported in the consolidated cash flow statement will depend upon the method of presentation of the statement. Where an entity prepares its cash flow statement under the direct method, only the cash dividends received from associated undertakings will be shown under operating or investing activities in line with the group's policy for dividends received. Under the indirect method, the starting point is net profit or loss that will include the group's share of profits from associated undertakings. However, profit from associated undertakings does not give rise to any cash flow unless that profit is received in the form of dividends. So in order to reflect only the dividends received in the cash flow statement, the share of profits in associated undertakings will have to be deducted as a non-cash adjustment in the reconciliation of net profit or loss to operating cash flows (see worked example in chapter 13).

Investments accounted for on a proportional basis

8.7 Where a joint venture is included in the consolidated financial statements using proportional consolidation, the group's proportionate share of that joint venture's cash flows should be included in the consolidated cash flow statement on a line-by-line basis. [IAS 7 para 38]. Therefore, the proportionate share of the joint venture's cash flows from operating, investing and financing activities will be included in the consolidated cash flow statement. Adjustments may have to be made to eliminate cash transfers between the venturer and the joint venture to ensure that the cash flow statement reflects the external cash flows to the group only.

Acquisitions and disposals of subsidiaries

8.8   When a subsidiary undertaking (or other business unit) is acquired or disposed of during a financial year, the aggregate cash flows relating to the consideration should be reported separately under investing activities in the cash flow statement. [IAS 7 para 39]. A major acquisition or disposal should be disclosed separately on the face of the cash flow statement. Where acquisitions or disposals are not significant then the cash flows can be aggregated, however, the cash inflow from disposals must be presented separately from the cash outflow from acquisitions, as netting of these cash flows is not permitted.

8.9   The standard specifies the treatment of cash and cash equivalents acquired or transferred on acquisition or disposal of a subsidiary (or other business unit). The amounts of cash and cash equivalents paid or received in respect of the consideration should be shown under investing activities *net* of any cash and cash equivalents balances transferred as part of the purchase or sale. [IAS 7 para 42].

8.10   Recording the consideration cash flows net of any cash and cash equivalents balances transferred means that any fixed assets, working capital excluding cash and cash equivalents and borrowings of the subsidiary at the date of acquisition or disposal, would need to be eliminated from other cash flow headings so as to avoid double counting. For example, inventory, debtors and creditors acquired or disposed of would need to be eliminated from the total balance sheet changes in inventory, debtors and creditors in the reconciliation of net profit to operating cash flows when reporting under the indirect method. The worked example at the end of the chapter shows the adjustments that need to be made for an acquisition.

8.11   Where the consideration for the acquisition has been discharged partly in *cash* and partly by the issue of *shares*, the cash flow statement would show only the cash element of the consideration paid. This would be shown as a single item (net of any cash and cash equivalents of the subsidiary acquired) under investing activities. The shares that are issued as part of the consideration in exchange for net assets acquired do not give rise to any cash flows and, consequently, they should not be shown in the cash flow statement. Instead, they should be disclosed as non-cash transactions (see para 10.1).

Example

A parent company pays £20,000 in cash and issues £80,000 in shares to acquire a subsidiary with cash balances of £30,000 and other net assets including goodwill of £70,000. In this situation, the cash flow statement would show a net cash inflow of £10,000 under investing activities despite its being an acquisition.

8.12 Where acquisitions and disposals take place during a financial year the cash flows of the group should include the cash flows of the subsidiary for the same period as the group's income statement includes the subsidiary's results. This is rather obvious, but care should be taken to eliminate all cash flows between the group and the subsidiary acquired or disposed of for the period that the subsidiary is included within the consolidated figures.

8.13 The standard requires disclosures in respect of the cash flow effect of the acquisitions or disposals made in the financial year as follows:

- The *total* acquisition or disposal consideration.
- The amount of the acquisition or disposal consideration that comprises cash and cash equivalents.
- The amount of cash and cash equivalents in the subsidiary (or other business unit) transferred as a result of the acquisition or disposal (which will have been netted off against consideration in the form of cash and cash equivalents to give the net amount in cash flow statement – see para 8.9 above).
- The assets and liabilities (other than cash and cash equivalents) of the subsidiary acquired or disposed of, disclosed by each major category (see Table 7).

[IAS 7 para 40].

Table 7 – Disclosure of the effect of an acquisition

Agfa-Gevaert NV – Annual Report – 31 December 2002

4. Cash flow statements - effect of acquisitions

Acquisitions 2002

The acquisition of Mitra Inc. had the following effect on the Group's assets and liabilities:

MILLION EUROS	
Goodwill on acquisition	178
Property, plant and equipment	5
Inventories	1
Investments	2
Trade receivables	8
Other receivables	1
Cash and cash equivalents	15
Personnel liabilities	(1)
Trade accounts payable	(1)
Tax liabilities	(5)
Other liabilities	(6)
Minority interest	(4)
Consideration paid	**193**
Cash acquired	(15)
Net cash outflow	**178**

8.15 The standard is not clear whether these requirements apply for the acquisition or disposal of a subsidiary where the reporting entity is not preparing consolidated financial statements. Given that the purpose of the cash flow statement is to report the cash flows of the reporting entity, the entity accounts of the parent will not incorporate the cash flows of the subsidiary, therefore, reporting any cash consideration net of the cash transferred to or from the subsidiary would not accurately reflect the cash flows of the parent entity. Therefore, these disclosures are only required for the acquisition and disposal of subsidiaries in the consolidated financial statements. However, these disclosures are required in entity financial statements where they are in relation to the purchase or sale of a business unit or operation.

8.16 If a disposal meets the definition of a discontinuing operation in IAS 35, 'Discontinuing operations' then additional disclosure is required. A discontinuing operation is defined as:

"... *a component of an enterprise:*
(a) *that the enterprise, pursuant to a single plan, is:*
  (i)   *disposing of substantially in its entirety, such as by selling the component in a single transaction, by demerger or spin-off of ownership of the component to the enterprise's shareholders;*
  (ii) *disposing of piecemeal, such as by selling off the component's assets and settling its liabilities individually; or*
  (iii) *terminating through abandonment;*
(b) *that represents a separate major line of business or geographical area of operations; and*
(c) *that can be distinguished operationally and for financial reporting purposes."*

[IAS 35 para 2].

Entities are required to disclose the net cash flows in respect of the operating, investing and financing activities of a discontinuing operation. [IAS 35 para 27]. This disclosure is consistent with the separate disclosure in the income statement of the results of discontinuing operations required by IAS 35. There is no requirement to segregate cash inflows and cash outflows further under each of the three headings. An example of disclosure is given in Table 8.

Table 8 – Disclosure in respect of a discontinuing operation

Bayer AG – Annual Report – 31 December 2001

[6] Discontinuing operations

Bayer sold its 50 percent interest in EC Erdölchemie GmbH, Cologne, to the joint venture partner Deutsche BP AG, Hamburg, effective May 1, 2001. The operating result of Erdölchemie for 2001 shown in the following table comprises the result of the business group's operations up to the date of divestiture and the income from the sale of the 50 percent interest.

In April 2001 Bayer decided to divest the remaining activities of its Fibers Business Group, including the production facilities for Dorlastan® spandex fibers and Perlon® monofilaments.

In the course of its reorganization Bayer plans to divest the Haarmann & Reimerbusiness group, whose activities it now regards as non-core. It is therefore intended to sell the wholly owned subsidiary Haarmann & Reimer GmbH, a manufacturer of fragrances and flavors based in Holzminden, Germany.

The non-operating results and the income taxes attributable to Haarmann & Reimer, Fibers, Erdölchemie and DyStar are reflected in the corresponding items of the income statement.

A breakdown of the results of discontinuing operations is given below.

Euro million	Erdölchemie		Fibers		H & R		DyStar	Total	
	2001	2000	**2001**	2000	**2001**	2000	2000	**2001**	2000
Net sales	**233**	635	**232**	506	**872**	865	350	**1,337**	2,356
Cost of goods sold	**(196)**	(481)	**(205)**	(383)	**(481)**	(489)	(223)	**(882)**	(1,576)
Selling expenses	**(16)**	(45)	**(26)**	(50)	**(199)**	(197)	(68)	**(241)**	(360)
Research and development expenses	**(-)**	(2)	**(8)**	(9)	**(63)**	(54)	(9)	**(71)**	(74)
General administration Expenses	**(3)**	(9)	**(11)**	(8)	**(38)**	(39)	(21)	**(52)**	(77)

Other operating income	316	7	1	10	23	14	6	340	37
Other operating expenses	(1)	(6)	(20)	(15)	(41)	(32)	(30)	(62)	(83)
Operating result from discontinuing operations	333	99	(37)	51	73	68	5	369	223
Non-operating result	(1)	(1)	(1)	1	(4)	(6)	(18)	(6)	(24)
Income (Loss) before income taxes	332	98	(38)	52	69	62	(13)	363	199
Income taxes	(6)	-	(3)	(2)	(35)	(30)	1	(44)	(31)
Income (Loss) after taxes	326	98	(41)	50	34	32	(12)	319	168

[35] Discontinuing operations

Assets and liabilities include the following amounts pertaining to the discontinuing operations of Haarmann & Reimer and Fibers:

Euro million	Fibers		H & R		Erdöl-chemie	DyStar	Total	
	Dec 31 2001	Dec 31 2000	**Dec 31 2001**	Dec 31 2000	**Dec 31 2000**	Dec 31 2000	**Dec 31 2001**	Dec 31 2000
Noncurrent assets	**130**	143	**419**	423	**200**	89	**549**	855
Current assets (excluding liquid assets)	**99**	195	**384**	390	**199**	320	**483**	1,104
Liquid assets	**-**	-	**17**	30	**-**	11	**17**	41
Assets	**229**	338	**820**	843	**399**	420	**1,049**	2,000
Pension provisions	**28**	53	**74**	69	**59**	16	**102**	197
Other provisions	**17**	35	**43**	62	**39**	28	**60**	164
Financial obligations	**-**	-	**12**	15	**5**	76	**12**	96
Remaining liabilities	**29**	82	**104**	101	**59**	122	**133**	364
Liabilities	**74**	170	**233**	247	**162**	242	**307**	821

[42] Discontinuing operations

Discontinuing operations affected the Group cash flow statements as follows:

Euro million	Erdölchemie		Fibers		H & R		DyStar		Total
	2001	2000	**2001**	2000	**2001**	2000	2000	**2001**	2000
Net cash provided by operating activities	**13**	38	**28**	114	**118**	84	66	**159**	302
Net cash provided by (used in) investing activities	**474**	(87)	**(16)**	(30)	**(163)**	(116)	(65)	**295**	(298)
Net cash provided by (used in) financing activities	**0**	0	**(41)**	-	**77**	(7)	18	**36**	11
Change in cash and cash equivalents	**487**	(49)	**(29)**	84	**32**	(39)	19	**490**	15

Chapter 9

Foreign currency

9.1 An entity may engage in foreign currency activities in two main ways:

- First, it may enter directly into business transactions that are denominated in foreign currencies.
- Secondly, it may conduct its foreign operations through a subsidiary, associate, joint venture or branch whose operations are based or conducted in a country other than that of the investing company (a 'foreign operation').

9.2 The results of foreign currency transactions and the financial statements of the foreign operation will need to be translated into the currency in which the entity reports. This translation process should produce results that are compatible with the effect of exchange rate changes on an entity's cash flows and its equity. The accounting treatment of foreign currency operations in cash flow statements can be rather complex. The guidance that follow deals with the treatment of exchange differences in individual entities first, followed by their treatment in consolidated financial statements.

Individual entities

9.3 Where an individual entity has cash receipts or makes cash payments in a foreign currency, those receipts and payments should be translated into the reporting currency at the rate ruling at the date on which the cash receipt or payment is received or paid. [IAS 7 para 25]. IAS 21, 'The effects of changes in foreign exchange rates', permits the use of a weighted average rate for the period that approximates to the actual exchange rate to be used when recording transactions, for example, a monthly average. Therefore, for consistency, IAS 7 also permits such an approximate rate to be used for the purposes of the cash flow statement.

9.4   Exchange differences may arise because of a rate change between the transaction date (the date at which the transaction is recorded) and the settlement date. Exchange differences also arise where a transaction remains unsettled (that is, not realised in cash and cash equivalents) at the balance sheet date and is required to be retranslated at that date. Such differences relate to the retranslation of monetary assets and liabilities.

Settled transactions

9.5   Where a transaction is *settled* at an exchange rate that differs from that used when the transaction was initially recorded, the exchange difference will be recognised in the income statement in the period in which the settlement takes place. Where the direct method (see para 6.6) is used to present the cash flows from operating activities, the cash payment itself is presented and, therefore, any exchange differences between recognition and settlement do not cause any complications. However, where the indirect method is used, a reconciliation is required between net profit and operating cash flows. Any exchange gain or loss is already included in arriving at net profits and also has the effect of increasing or decreasing the reporting currency equivalent of amounts paid or received in cash settlement. Consequently no adjustment for the exchange gain or loss is necessary in the reconciliation of net profit to operating cash flows when the transaction is settled. Consider the following example:

Example

A UK company was set up in January 20X1 and raised £200,000 by issuing shares. It purchased goods for resale from France in February 20X1 for €200,000 when the exchange rate was £1 = €1.5. It entered the purchase in its inventory records as: €200,000 @ 1.5 = £133,333. Under the terms of the contract, the company settled the debt in October 200X1 when the exchange rate was £1 = €1.6. The amount paid in settlement was: €200,000 @ 1.6 = £125,000. The company would, therefore, record an exchange gain of £133,333 - £125,000 = £8,333 in arriving at its net profit for the year.

Assuming that there are no other transactions during the year and the inventory remained unsold at the balance sheet date at 31 December 20X1, a simplified cash flow statement is given below:

Cash flow statement

	£	£
Cash flows from operating activities		
Net profit	8,333	
Adjustment for:		
Increase in inventories	(133,333)	
Net cash flow used in operating activities		(125,000)
Cash flows from financing activities		
Issue of shares	200,000	
Net cash flow from financing activities		200,000
Net increase in cash and cash equivalents*		75,000
Working		
Proceeds for share issue		200,000
Less : payments for inventory		(125,000)
Net increase in cash and cash equivalents		75,000

It is obvious that the net cash flow used in operating activities comprises the payment of £125,000 for the inventory. Because the outstanding creditor for £133,333 was settled during the year for £125,000, the exchange gain of £8,333 is already reflected in the payment and, therefore, no adjustment for the exchange gain is necessary in reconciling the net profit to operating cash flow as illustrated above. Therefore, as a general rule, exchange differences on settled transactions relating to operations will not appear as a reconciling item in the reconciliation of net profit to net cash flow from operating activities for the indirect method.

*Represented by closing cash balances

9.6 Where a settled transaction does not relate to operating activities and the exchange gain or loss is included in the income statement, the exchange gain or loss should be removed in the reconciliation required under the indirect method as it will in effect be included as part of the cash flows arising from the settlement disclosed under investing or financing activities. An example would be dividend income from a foreign investment shown under investing activities as dividends received. In this situation, the sterling equivalent of foreign cash actually received would be shown under investing activities and would reflect any exchange gain or loss that arises at the time of receipt and reported in the income statement.

Unsettled transactions

9.7 Where the transaction remains *outstanding* at the balance sheet date, an exchange difference arises as a consequence of recording the foreign currency transaction at the rate ruling at the date of the transaction (or when it was translated at a previous balance sheet date) and the subsequent retranslation to the rate ruling at the balance sheet date. This exchange difference will generally be included in the income statement. Normally such exchange differences arise on monetary items (for example, foreign currency loans, debtors and creditors). In the context of an individual company's operations, these exchange gains or losses will ultimately be reflected in cash flows. However, the way in which they affect the cash flow statement will depend upon the nature of the monetary assets or liabilities, that is, whether they are used in relation to operating, investing or financing activities.

9.8 Again where the direct method is used to present operating cash flows, the cash payment itself is reflected, therefore, any exchange difference can be ignored in preparing the cash flow statement. Where the indirect method is used, the exchange differences that arise on translation at the balance sheet date for monetary items that form part of operating activities, such as debtors and creditors, will require no adjustment in the reconciliation of net profit to net cash flow from operating activities, even though they do not involve any cash flows. This is because increases or decreases in the debtor or creditor balances will include the exchange differences on their retranslation at the balance sheet date, which would be offset against their equivalent exchange gain or loss included in net profit for the year. The effect is that the net cash flow from operating activities will not be distorted by such retranslation differences as illustrated in the following example.

Example

The facts are the same as in the previous example except that at the company's year end 31 December 20X1 the account had not been settled. At 31 December 20X1 the exchange rate was £1 = €1.55 so that the original creditor for £133,333 would be retranslated at €200,000 @ 1.55 = £129,032. The gain on exchange of £133,333- £129,032 = £4,301 would be reported as part of net profit for the year. The cash flow statement would be as follows:

Cash flow statement	**£**	**£**
Cash flows from operating activities		
Net profit	4,301	
Adjustments for:		
Increase in inventories	(133,333)	
Increase in creditors	129,032	
Net cash flow from operating activities		Nil
Cash flows from financing activities		
Issue of shares	200,000	
Net cash flow from financing activities		200,000
Net increase in cash and cash equivalents*		200,000

It is clear that the exchange difference included in net profit and in the year end creditor balance cancel each other with the result that cash flow from operating activities is not affected and no adjustment is required in the reconciliation.

9.9 Therefore, as a general rule, balance sheet movements in foreign currency trade debtors and creditors, except where they relate to foreign

---

*Represented by closing cash balances

subsidiaries (see para 9.18 below), will include the impact of exchange differences reported in net profit and no adjustments for such exchange differences are strictly necessary in the reconciliation. It should be noted, however, that some entities prefer to split the movement on the debtors/creditors into cash, foreign exchange, acquisitions and other movements, including only the movement in cash in the reconciliation. In this case, then the exchange gain or loss included in arriving at net profit will not be offset by the total movement in debtors or creditors and, therefore, must be adjusted for the reconciliation to balance.

9.10 Exchange differences on monetary items that form part of investing or financing activities such as long-term loans will normally be reported as part of the net profit or loss for the financial year. They need to be eliminated in arriving at the net cash flows from operating activities when performing the reconciliation for the indirect method. This is rather obvious, because the actual movement on long-term monetary items that includes the relevant exchange difference is not reported in the reconciliation of net profit to operating cash flow as they are not operating activity items. Consider the following example:

Example

The opening balance sheet at 1 October 20X1 of a company consists of cash of £100,000 and share capital of £100,000. The company takes out a long-term loan on 31 March 20X2 of US$270,000 when the rate of exchange is £1 = US$1.4. The proceeds are immediately converted to sterling, that is, £192,857. There are no other transactions during the year. The exchange rate at the balance sheet date 30 September 20X2 is £1 = US$1.6.

The summarised balance sheet at 30 September 20X2

	£000	£000
Assets		
Cash		293
Total assets		293
Equity and liabilities		
Capital and reserves		
Share capital	100	
Reserves	24	
		124
Non-current liabilities		
Long-term loan ($270,000 @ 1.6)		169
Total equity and liabilities		293

The foreign currency loan having been translated at the rate ruling at the date of receipt to £192,857 (US$270,000 @ 1.4), is retranslated at the balance sheet date to £168,750 (US$270,000 @ 1.6). The exchange gain of £24,107 is recognised in net profit for the year. The cash is made up of £100,000 received from the share issue and £192,857 received on converting the currency loan immediately to sterling.

Cash flow statement

	£000	£000
Cash flows from operating activities		
Net profit	24	
Adjustment for:		
Foreign exchange gain	(24)	
Net cash flow from operating activities		Nil
Cash flows from financing activities		
Receipt of foreign currency loan	193	
Net cash flow from financing activities		193
Net increase in cash and cash equivalents		193
Cash and cash equivalents at beginning of period		100
Cash and cash equivalents at end of period*		293

*Represented by year end cash balances.

It is apparent from the above illustration that the exchange loss of £24,107 does not have any cash flow effect and is related to financing activities. Therefore, it needs to be eliminated from net profit. A similar adjustment would be necessary if the loan remains outstanding at 30 September 20X3.

9.11 Where exchange differences arise on the retranslation of foreign currency cash and cash equivalent balances themselves, these are not cash flows, however, they should be reported in the cash flow statement in order to reconcile opening and closing balances of cash and cash equivalents (see paras 5.3 and 7.2). This amount should be presented separately from operating, financing or investing cash flows. [IAS 7 para 28].

Group entities

9.12 Where a group conducts part of its business through a foreign operation, different considerations arise from those for individual transactions discussed above. This is because the cash flows of the foreign operation are considered as a whole rather than as a series of single transactions. There are two commonly accepted methods of translation, the first is adopted where the foreign operations are integral to the operations of the reporting entity (known as the temporal method in the UK) whilst the second, more common, method is used for foreign entities, that is where the foreign operations are not integral to the entity (similar to the closing rate method in the UK).

Foreign operations integral to the entity

9.13 Where foreign operations are integral to the entity, all non-monetary items and income statement items of the foreign operation are translated at the rate ruling on the transaction date or at an average rate for a period if this is not materially different. [IAS 21 paras 27, 9,11]. As a result the only exchange differences that arise will be those relating to monetary items which are retranslated at the closing rate. These exchange differences will be reported in the income statement.

9.14 By using this method, the consolidated financial statements reflect the transactions of the foreign operation as if they had been entered into by the reporting entity itself. Accordingly, the treatment of foreign currency cash flow transactions and exchange differences in the consolidated cash flow statement will be similar to that explained above for individual companies.

Foreign entities

9.15 Where the foreign operation is not integral to the entity, it is known as a 'foreign entity' under IAS 21. The method of translation for foreign entities under IAS 21 requires monetary and non-monetary assets and liabilities to be translated at the closing rate and income and expense items to be translated at the rate ruling at the date of the transaction or an average rate which approximates to the actual exchange rates, for example, an average rate for the period. All exchange differences are taken to equity, until disposal of the foreign entity when they are recycled to the income statement. [IAS 21 paras 30, 31]. IAS 7 requires that the cash flow statement of a subsidiary should be translated at the date of transaction or an average rate in line with the income statement treatment above.

9.16 Where a foreign operation is treated as a 'foreign entity', then all exchange differences relating to the retranslation of the opening net assets of the foreign entity to the closing rate will have been taken directly to reserves. As such exchange differences have no actual or prospective cash flow effect, they will not be included in the consolidated cash flow statement. However, where the opening net assets include foreign currency cash and cash equivalents, then, to that extent, the exchange difference arising on their retranslation at the closing rate for the current period will have been reflected in the closing balances. Such translation differences should be reported in the cash flow statement to determine the total movement in cash and cash equivalents in the period (see paras 5.3 and 7.2).

9.17 Where the group translates the foreign entity's income statement at an average rate, a further translation difference between the result translated at the average rate and the result translated at the closing rate will be taken to reserves. This difference will include the exchange rate effect of the movement in foreign currency cash and cash equivalents from the average rate to the closing rate. This exchange difference will be included with the exchange differences arising on the retranslation of the opening foreign currency cash and cash equivalents (as stated in the preceding paragraph) in the cash flow statement.

9.18 The treatment of foreign currency exchange differences in the consolidated cash flow statement can be fairly complex and the following example illustrates the application of the principles discussed above.

Example

Company A, a UK company, whose accounting period ended on 30 September 20X2, has a wholly-owned US subsidiary, S corporation, that was acquired for US$600,000 on 30 September 20X1. The fair value of the net assets at the date of acquisition was US$500,000. The exchange rate at 30 September 20X1 and 20X2 was £1 = US$2.0 and £1 = US$1.5 respectively. The average rate for the year ended 30 September 20X2 was £1 = US$1.65

The summarised balance sheet at 30 September 20X1 and 20X2, an analysis of the net profit for the year ended 30 September 20X2 and the statement of changes in equity for the year ended 30 September 20X2 of S corporation, extracted from the consolidation returns, in dollars and sterling equivalents, are as follows:

Balance sheets of S corporation

	20X2 $'000	20X1 $'000	20X2 £'000 Closing $1.50	20X1 £'000 Closing $2.00
Assets				
Non-current assets				
Property, plant and equipment:				
Cost (20X2 additions; $30)	255	225	170.0	112.5
Depreciation (20X2 charge: $53)	(98)	(45)	(65.3)	(22.5)
Net book value	157	180	104.7	90.0
Current assets				
Investments	250	100	166.6	50.0
Inventories	174	126	116.0	63.0
Debtors	210	145	140.0	72.5
Cash and cash equivalents	240	210	160.0	105.0
	874	581	582.6	290.5
Total assets	1,031	761	687.3	380.5
Equity and liabilities				
Capital and reserves				
Share capital	300	300	150.0	150.0
Reserves				
Pre acquisition	200	200	100.0	100.0
Post acquisition	76	-	46.6	-
Exchange differences	-	-	87.4	-
	576	500	384.0	250.0
Current liabilities				
Bank overdraft	150	-	100.0	-
Trade creditors	125	113	83.3	56.5
Taxation	30	18	20.0	9.0
	305	131	203.3	65.5
Non-current liabilities				
Loan stock	150	130	100.0	65.0
Total equity and liabilities	1,031	761	687.3	380.5

S corporation
Analysis of net profit for the year ended 30 September 20X2

	$'000	£'000
		Average
		$1.65
Profit from operations	135	81.8
Interest paid	(15)	(9.1)
Taxation	(30)	(18.1)
Net profit for the period	90	54.6

Working

Exchange difference:	
Total opening assets ($761/1.5 - $761/2)	126.8
Total opening liabilities ($261/1.5 - $261/2)	(43.5)
Net profit for the year ($90/1.5 - $90/1.65)	5.4
Dividends ($14/1.5 - $14/1.75*)	(1.3)
	87.4

S corporation
Statement of changes in equity

	$'000 Share capital	$'000 Accu-mulated profits	$'000 Total	£'000 Share capital	£'000 Accu-mulated profits	£'000 Trans-lation reserve	£'000 Total
Balance as at 1 October 20X1	300	200	500	150	100.0	-	250.0
Currency translation differences	-	-	-	-	-	87.4	87.4
Net gains not recognised in the income statement	-	-	-	-	-	87.4	87.4
Net profit for the period	-	90	90	-	54.6	-	54.6
Dividends paid for 20X1	-	(14)	(14)	-	(8.0)	-	(8.0)
Balance at 30 September 20X2	300	276	576	150	146.6	87.4	384.0

*Actual rate on date dividend received

It is further assumed that company A does not trade on its own and its only income is dividends received from S corporation. The summarised balance sheet of company A at 30 September 20X1 and 20X2 is as follows:

Company A Balance sheets

	20X2 £'000	20X1 £'000
Assets		
Non-current assets		
Investment in subsidiary ($600,000 @ 2.0)	300	300
Current assets		
Cash	208	200
Total assets	508	500
Equity		
Share capital	500	500
Accumulated profits (dividend received $14000 @ 1.75*)	8	-
Total equity	508	500

Where company A regards S corporation as a foreign entity, it must use the average rate for translating the income statement of S corporation. The summarised consolidated income statement for the year ended 30 September 20X2 and the summarised consolidated balance sheet at that date are as follows:

Consolidated income statement for the year ended 30 September 20X2

	£'000
Net profit of company A	8.0
Net profit of S corporation	54.6
	62.6
Adjustment for intercompany dividend	(8.0)
Net profit for the period	54.6

---

*Actual rate on date dividend received

Consolidated balance sheet as at 30 September 20X2

		£'000
Assets		
Non-current assets		
Property, plant and equipment		104.7
Goodwill ($100,000 @ 1.5)		66.7
Current assets		
Investments	166.6	
Inventories	116.0	
Debtors	140.0	
Cash and cash equivalents		
(Company A £208, S corporation £160)	368.0	790.6
Total Assets		962.0
Equity and liabilities		
Capital and reserves		
Share capital	500.0	
Accumulated profits	54.6	
Translation reserve (see below)	104.1	658.7
Current liabilities		
Bank overdraft	100.0	
Trade creditors	83.3	
Taxation	20.0	203.3
Non-current liabilities		
Loan stock		100.0
Total equity and liabilities		962.0

In the above illustration goodwill has been treated as a currency asset, which is retranslated at the closing rate. Therefore, the translation reserve stated above comprises the exchange difference relating to the subsidiary as previously calculated of £874,000 and a further exchange difference arising on the retranslation of the goodwill of £167,000 ($200,000 @ 2.0 - $200,000 @ 1.5), a total of £1,041,000.

Given the above information, the consolidated cash flow statement drawn up using the average rate for the year and the related notes to the cash flow statement are as follows:

Consolidated cash flow statement for the year ended 30 September 20X2

		£'000	£'000
Cash flows from operating activities			
Net profit		54.6	
Adjustments for:			
Depreciation	($53,000 @ 1.65)	32.1	
Interest expense		9.1	
Tax expense		18.1	
Increase in inventories	($48,000 @ 1.65)	(29.1)	
Increase in debtors	($65,000 @ 1.65)	(39.4)	
Increase in creditors	($12,000 @ 1.65)	7.3	
Cash generated from operations		52.7	
Interest paid	($15,000 @ 1.65)	(9.1)	
Taxation paid	($18,000 @ 1.65)	(10.9)	
Net cash flow from operating activities			32.7
Cash flows from investing activities			
Purchase of property, plant and equipment	($30,000 @ 1.65)	(18.1)	
Purchase of current asset investments	($150,000 @ 1.65)	(90.9)	
Net cash flow used in investing activities			(109.0)
Cash flows from financing activities			
Issue of loan stock	($20,000 @ 1.65)	12.1	
Net cash flow from financing activities			12.1
Effects of exchange rates on cash and cash equivalents (see workings below)			27.2
Net decrease in cash and cash equivalents			(37.0)
Cash and cash equivalents at the beginning of the period			305.0
Cash and cash equivalents at the end of the period			268.0

Notes to the cash flow statement

1. Cash and cash equivalents

Cash and cash equivalents consist of cash in hand balances and bank overdrafts repayable on demand. Cash and cash equivalents included in the cash flow statement comprise the following balance sheet amounts:

	20X2 £'000	20X1 £'000
Cash in hand balances	368	305
Bank overdrafts	(100)	-
Cash and cash equivalents	268	305

(Note - The comparative cash in hand balance of £305,000 is made up of cash and cash equivalents in S corporation of £105,000 ($210,000 @ 2) and in company A of £200,000.)

The effect of the foreign exchange rate changes on the cash and cash equivalents balance is calculated as follows:

Effects of exchange rates on foreign currency cash and cash equivalents

		£'000
Cash at bank		
Opening balance	($210 @ 1.5 - $210 @ 2.0)	35.0
Increase	($30 @ 1.5 - $30 @ 1.65)	1.8
Bank overdraft		
Opening balance		-
Increase	($150 @ 1.5 - $150 @ 1.65)	(9.1)
Exchange difference on inter-company dividend (see para 35.142)	($14 @ 1.75 - $14 $ 1.65)	(0.5)
Effects of exchange rates on cash and cash equivalents		27.2

The exchange differences arising on retranslation of other net assets (for example, the current asset investments and the loan stock) do not affect the cash flow statement as they are non-cash items. Also, as they have been taken to equity as part of the exchange difference arising on retranslation of S corpation's net assets, they are not included in net profit and so do not appear in the reconciliation of net profit to operating cash flows. However, the exchange differences on cash and cash equivalents, whilst also being taken to equity as part of the exchange difference arising on retranslation of S corpation's net assets, are included in the cash flow statement as part of the reconciliation of opening to closing cash and cash equivalents (see paras 5.3 and 7.2).

The movement in working capital in arriving at operating cash flows can also be obtained by taking the difference between the closing and the opening balance sheet figures and adjusting the result to eliminate the non-cash effects of exchange rate adjustments, but this method is rather cumbersome as illustrated below for inventories.

		£'000
Stocks at 30 September 20X2	($174 @ 1.5)	116.0
Stocks at 30 September 20X1	($126 @ 2.0)	63.0
Increase in stocks ($48)		53.0
Exchange difference:		
On opening balance ($126 @ 1.5 - $126 @ 2.0)		(21.0)
On movement ($48 @ 1.5 - $48 @ 1.65)		(2.9)
Increase in stocks as per		
reconciliation above		29.1

If the full movement in inventories of £53,000 is used for the reconciliation, a further adjustment would be required in the reconciliation to eliminate the £23,900 exchange movement.

9.19   As can be seen from the above example, in practice, a reporting entity will find it simpler to require each of its foreign subsidiaries to prepare a cash flow statement with supporting notes, in its domestic currency. This cash flow statement can then be translated into sterling. The sterling equivalent of each subsidiary's cash flow statement can then be consolidated with the cash flow statement of the reporting entity after eliminating intra-group items such as dividends and inter-group loans.

Intra-group transactions

9.20   Transactions between members of a group located in different countries may not cancel out on consolidation because of exchange differences. These exchange differences are usually reported in the income statement, particularly if they relate to intra-group trading transactions. Such exchange differences may have an effect on group cash flows. For consolidated cash flow statements, these intra-group cash flows may not cancel out unless the actual rate at the date of transfer is used for translation. In the previous example, the only intra-group transaction that took place between the parent and the subsidiary was in respect of a dividend payment. The dividend paid by the subsidiary in respect of the previous year has been translated for consolidated purposes at the rate of exchange on the date of the cash receipt ($14,000 @ 1.75 = £8,000) and also recorded at that rate by the parent and, hence, no exchange difference arose in the consolidated profit and loss account. However, this does not mean that the exchange difference has been eliminated in the cash flow statement. The effect of using the actual amount received in the cancellation process means that the profits remitted by the subsidiary are being translated at the average rate. As a result the intra-group dividend paid and received does not cancel out in the consolidated cash flow statement. The difference of £500 ($14,000 @1.75 - $14,000 @1.65) needs to be adjusted. The standard states that the effect of exchange rate changes on cash and cash equivalents held or due in foreign currency is reported in the cash flow statement in order to reconcile cash and cash equivalents at the beginning and end of the period. [IAS 7 para 28]. It could be argued that it makes more sense to report this exchange rate difference in the reconciliation of net profit to operating cash flows. This is because the subsidiary's cash has gone down by £8,500 and the parent company's cash has gone up by £8,000, resulting in a real economic loss to the group that normally falls to be recognised in the consolidated profit and loss account. However, the treatment required by the standard ensures that the profit and loss account and the cash flow statement are treated in a consistent way. Because, in the above example, net profit does not include any exchange difference on the intra-group dividend, it follows that no adjustment for the exchange difference is necessary in the reconciliation of net profit to operating cash flows. The only other place to report this exchange difference is in the movement that reconciles opening balance of cash and cash equivalents to the closing balance as shown in the above example.

Cash flows from hedging activities

9.21 Hedging transactions are normally undertaken by entities to protect them from financial loss, especially loss that would occur if prices or exchange rates were to vary. For example, an entity may purchase or sell a hedging instrument, such as a futures contract or a forward contract, in order to protect itself from price fluctuations that may arise in connection with the sale or purchase of inventory. The question arises as to how cash flows that result from the purchase or sale of the hedging instrument should be classified in the cash flow statement. Should these be shown under investing activities or classified in the same category as the cash flows of the items being hedged, for example, under operating activities?

9.22 IAS 7 provides that cash flows that result from transactions undertaken to hedge another transaction should be classified in the same manner as the transactions that are the subject of the hedge. [IAS 7 para 16]. This is a sensible treatment, because it links the cash flows from hedging instruments that are accounted for as hedges with the cash flows arising from the items being hedged. The treatment required by the standard for hedging transactions should only apply to financial instruments such as futures contracts, forward contracts, options and swaps, that have been appropriately identified as a hedge of an identifiable position in accordance with IAS 39, 'Financial instruments: Recognition and measurement'. For example, the reporting entity may purchase a futures contract in order to reduce its exposure to increases in the price of a planned inventory purchase. Cash flows in relation to the futures contract would be classified as an operating activity cash flow, which is consistent with the treatment of the inventory purchase.

9.23 The treatment required by IAS 7 for hedged transactions cannot apply to situations where the reporting entity hedges a net investment in a foreign subsidiary with a borrowing that is denominated in the same currency as the net investment being hedged. Accounting for the borrowing as a hedge is incidental; it cannot change the basic fact that it is still a borrowing. Furthermore, the foreign subsidiary may have

Foreign currency

contributed to group cash flows reported under each of the standard headings. Since the cash flows from the borrowings cannot be identified with any specific cash flows from that subsidiary, it follows that the cash flows from the borrowing can only be classified in the cash flow statement under financing.

Chapter 10

Notes to the cash flow statement

Specific disclosures

10.1 In addition to the cash flow statement itself, IAS 7 requires a number of explanatory notes to the cash flow statements. Many of the specific disclosures that are necessary to supplement the information presented in the cash flow statement have already been discussed elsewhere in this chapter, but are given below for completeness.

- Where operating cash flows are reported under the indirect method, the net profit or loss has to be reconciled to the cash flow from operating activities. This reconciliation may be presented on the face of the cash flow statement or in a note (see para 6.9). [IAS 7 para 20].
- The components of cash and cash equivalents used for the purposes of the cash flow statement should be disclosed in a note, together with a reconciliation of these amounts to the relevant balance sheet items (see para 7.1). IAS 7 notes that in order to comply with IAS 1, 'Presentation of financial statements', an entity should disclose the policy that it adopts in determining the composition of cash and cash equivalents. [IAS 7 paras 45, 46].
- Where a group acquires or disposes of a subsidiary undertaking (or other business unit) specific disclosures are required in relation to the cash flow effect (see para 8.13), being:
  - The total acquisition or disposal consideration, together with how much of the consideration comprised cash and cash equivalents.
  - The amount of the cash and cash equivalents in the subsidiary (or other business unit) transferred as a result of the acquisition or disposal.

- The assets and liabilities (other than cash and cash equivalents) of the subsidiary acquired or disposed of, by each major category (see Table 7).

[IAS para 40].

- Non-cash investing and financing activity transactions should also be disclosed in a note to the accounts. [IAS 7 para 43]. Such transactions do not involve any cash flow, but have the same effect as if several cash transactions were made together. For example, conversion of debt to equity can be viewed as the equivalent of repaying debt in cash and then receiving cash on the issue of new shares. However, because there are no actual cash flows, the transaction would not feature in the cash flow statement. Important information would thereby remain undisclosed merely because, in effect, a notional cash outflow has been cancelled by an equal and opposite notional cash inflow. Therefore, in order to report the activities of an entity in full, material non-cash transactions should be disclosed in a note to the cash flow statement in order to provide all the relevant information about these transactions. Other examples of non-cash transactions given in IAS 7 are the acquisition of assets either by assuming directly-related liabilities or by means of a finance lease and the acquisition of an entity by means of an equity issue. [IAS 7 para 44].

- Where a significant amount of cash and cash equivalent balances are not available for use by the group, disclosure is required of the relevant amounts along with a commentary on their restriction. [IAS 7 para 48]. Sometimes cash may be held in a separate blocked account or an escrow account to be used only for a specific purpose, or held by subsidiaries operating in countries where exchange control restrictions are in force, such that cash is not freely transferable around the group. A typical example of disclosure is where a foreign subsidiary is prevented from remitting funds to its overseas parent, because of local exchange control regulations. Other examples where disclosure may be relevant, depending on the regulatory environment, relate to cash balances in escrow, deposited with a regulator or held within an employee share ownership trust. The treatment of restricted cash is dealt with in paragraph 11.16 below.

• Entities are required to disclose the net cash flows in respect of the operating, investing and financing activities of a discontinuing operation (see para 8.16 and Table 8). [IAS 35 para 27].

Supplementary disclosures

10.2 In addition to the specific disclosures identified above, the standard *encourages* reporting entities to provide any additional information that will aid users in understanding the entity's financial position and liquidity. Some additional information encouraged to be presented by the standard is considered below.

Undrawn facilities

10.3 Entities are encouraged to disclose the amount of any undrawn borrowing facilities to users, for example, undrawn loan facility agreed with the bank. Disclosure of any restrictions on the use of these facilities by the entity is also encouraged. [IAS 7 para 50(a)].

Cash flows from entities accounted for using proportional consolidation

10.4 Disclosure of the cash flows arising from those investments accounted for as joint ventures using proportional consolidation is encouraged. The aggregate cash flows for each of the three main classifications of operating, investing and financing activities would provide useful information to users. [IAS 7 para 50(b)].

Cash flows from operating activities

10.5 The standard encourages entities to give separate disclosure of those operating cash flows that represent maintaining the entity's operating capacity and those that represent an increase in the entity's operating capacity. [IAS 7 para 50(c)]. This information will assist users in assessing the entity's investment in operating activity in the business with a view to the future profitability of the business.

Segmental cash flows

10.6   IAS 14, 'Segment reporting', requires the disclosure of certain items reported in the financial statements by business and geographical segment. IAS 7 encourages that cash flows should also be reported on this basis, suggesting that operating, financing and investing activities be reported by segment. [IAS 7 para 50(d)]. This enables users to understand the relationship between the cash flows of the business as a whole and those of its component parts. IAS 7 does not specifically identify the type of segmental cash flow information to be reported, but as a minimum an entity should consider giving an analysis of the most important elements of operating cash flows between the major reportable segments. Clearly, there may be problems of allocation, such as common costs and interest, but they could be allocated between segments in the same way as other segmental information. An example of a company that has given a segmental analysis of operating, investing and financing cash flows is shown in Table 9.

Table 9 – Segmental analysis of cash flows by business segment

FLS Industries A/S – Annual Report – 31 December 2002

1. Breakdown of the Group by core businesses in 2002 (extract)

DKKm	F.L.Smidth Group	FLS Building Materials [1]	FLS miljo APC activity [2]	Other companies etc. [3]	Core activities	Non-strategic activities [4]	FLS Group
CASH FLOWS							
Cash flows from operating activities	234	539	27	134	934	(220)	714
Acquisition and disposal of undertakings and activities	18	59	0	(101)	(24)	691	667
Additions of tangible fixed assets	(114)	(290)	(3)	(1)	(408)	(225)	(633)
Other investments	(11)	192	0	68	249	693	942
Cash flows from investing activities	(107)	(39)	(3)	(34)	(183)	1,159	976
Cash flows from operating and investing activities	127	500	24	100	751	939	1,690
Cash flows from financing activities	(462)	(467)	(50)	64	(915)	(695)	(1,610)
Change in cash funds	(335)	33	(26)	164	(164)	244	80

Reconciliation of cash and cash equivalents to net debt

10.7 UK companies are required under FRS 1 to provide a reconciliation of net cash flow to net debt, which they regard as more useful than the movement in cash and cash equivalents in providing a better understanding of the liquidity and solvency of their businesses. Paragraph 50 of IAS 7 encourages disclosure of additional information relevant to users in understanding the financial position and liquidity of the entity together with a commentary by management. Although a reconciliation to net debt is not one of the examples given by the standard, there is nothing in the standard to prevent an entity from giving a reconciliation of cash and cash equivalents to net debt, which can provide useful information about changes in liquidity on a broader basis that that provided solely by the movement in cash and cash equivalent balances.

10.8 Under FRS 1, the reconciliation is given adjoining the cash flow statement (for example, at the foot of the cash flow statement) or as a note to it. We believe that the reconciliation could be given in a similar way under IAS 7 – either on the face of the cash flow statement, but clearly labelled and kept separate to reflect the fact that it is not part of the cash flow statement or in the notes. There is nothing in IAS 7 to suggest that information cannot be shown on the face of the cash flow statement. Furthermore, the exposure draft to IAS 1 says, *"This Standard sometimes uses the term 'disclosure' in a broad sense, encompassing items presented on the face of each financial statement as well as in the notes to the financial statements. Disclosures also are required by other International Financial Reporting Standards and Interpretations of those Standards. Unless specified to the contrary in this Standard, another Standard or an Interpretation of a Standard, such disclosures are made on the face of the relevant financial statement or in the notes"*. [ED IAS 1 para 41]. Therefore, those UK companies that present the reconciliation of net debt at the foot of the cash flow statement can continue to do so under IAS 7.

Commentary on cash flows in operating and financial review

10.9 As stated in paragraph 10.7, IAS 7 encourages disclosure of additional information relevant to users in understanding the financial position and liquidity of the entity together with a commentary by management. [IAS 7 para 50]. Therefore, UK companies may continue to provide additional information that is recommended by the ASB's voluntary statement 'Operating and financial review' (OFR). The OFR provides opportunities for listed companies and other large corporations where there is a public interest in their financial statements to provide a commentary on their cash flows. The OFR recommends discussion in the 'financial review' section of 'cash flows' and 'current liquidity'. Many UK companies may continue to take advantage of this opportunity to provide further information on their cash generating potential and liquidity position that go beyond that required and encouraged by IAS 7.

10.10 For example, the OFR encourages companies to disclose and discuss segmental cash flows where they are significantly out of line with segmental profits, because of the impact of capital expenditure. [OFR para 33]. In fact, IAS 7 also encourages entities to give a segmental breakdown of their cash flows, but does not specify how this information should be given. This is dealt with in paragraph 10.6 above.

10.11 Some companies also disclose 'cash flow per share'. Although some may argue that disclosure of cash flow per share should not be given on the grounds that it could be regarded as comparable to earnings per share and could be regarded as a substitute for it, there is, in principle, nothing wrong with disclosing this information. Indeed, there is no such prohibition in IAS 7. Cash flow per share information presented over time would reveal the trend of cash flows and, when compared to earnings per share, would demonstrate the quality of profits earned.

10.12 In discussing current liquidity, the OFR calls for disclosure and comments on the level of borrowings including seasonality, peak borrowing levels and maturity profile of both borrowings and committed borrowing facilities. [OFR para 34]. At present, financial statement disclosure about actual borrowings at the year end is provided by analysing bank and other borrowings by maturity period of up to one year, one to two years, two to five years and beyond five years. In addition, as stated in paragraph 10.3 above, IAS 7 encourages entities to disclose the amount of undrawn borrowing facilities (both committed and uncommitted). Disclosure of an entity's borrowing facilities together with its ability to access further resources will, no doubt, go a long way in providing useful information about the entity's viability and financial adaptability. However, the level of disclosure is left entirely to the company for obvious reasons. For example, companies could resist such disclosure on the grounds that it provides too much competitive information. Also the company's main bankers could object, because disclosure may provide competitors with valuable information on their lending policies.

10.13 The discussion on borrowings suggested by the OFR should also refer to any restrictions on the ability of the group to transfer funds from one part of the group to another and restrictions and breaches of borrowing covenants. [OFR paras 36, 37]. The disclosure of the amounts of cash that are not freely remittable to the parent company coupled with sufficient information on the restrictions (for example, exchange controls) provides useful information for users of financial statements to make an assessment of the probable future effect of the restriction on the company's cash flows. Indeed, IAS 7 specifically requires this type of disclosure as discussed in paragraph 10.1 above. Similarly, information on assets and liabilities denominated in foreign currencies, which incidentally is not directly relevant for supplementing information reported in the cash flow statement, may be useful for making assessments of a company's financial position and liquidity. Information on any restrictive financial covenants on current borrowing agreements and breaches or likely breaches of covenants is equally important in assessing its viability and financial adaptability.

Comparative figures

10.14 IAS 1, 'Presentation of financial statements', requires that comparative figures should be given for all numerical information reported in the financial statements, unless a standard permits or requires otherwise. Therefore, comparative figures are required for all items reported in the cash flow statement and in the supplementary notes. However, paragraph 40 of IAS 7 only requires disclosure of additional information in relation to the acquisition or disposal of a subsidiary in the period in which the transaction takes place. No reference is made as to whether comparative information should be given since the standard does not specifically deal with the presentation of comparative information. Many companies do not provide such comparative information, although it is arguable that where an acquisition or disposal has taken place both in the current and the preceding year, such additional information should be given for both years.

Chapter 11

Practical application

11.1   This section attempts to clarify some of the practical problems that may arise in interpreting and applying IAS 7.

Commercial paper programmes

11.2   Many large industrial and commercial companies raise funds by issuing commercial paper in the form of unsecured promissory notes with fixed maturity between seven and 364 days. Often these are backed up by committed bank facilities. Normally these are issued at a discount to the face value and provide a cheaper source of finance than other means of borrowing.

11.3   Where a company has in place a commercial paper programme that involves issues and redemptions throughout the financial year, the question arises as to how these potentially large inflows and outflows should be shown in the cash flow statement. For transactions of this nature, the reporting of the net change in the obligation in the financing activity section of the cash flow statement is permitted provided the maturities are short (less than three months), the turnover is quick and the volume of transactions is large (see para 5.15). [IAS 7 para 22(b)]. The alternative of showing the gross amounts for raising and repaying money under the commercial paper programme would not add very much to users' understanding of the company's financing activities.

Discounts and premiums

11.4   The standard does not specifically address how the redemption of a deep discounted bond or the premium payable on the redemption of a debt security should be treated in the cash flow statement. Under IAS 39, 'Financial instruments: Recognition and measurement', the liability will be measured at amortised cost. Any difference between the initial measurement at cost (being the fair value of the consideration received) and the maturity value of the liability, such as a discount or a redemption premium, will be amortised to the income statement as a finance cost. Such finance costs are similar to interest costs for the liability and, therefore, the cash flow effects of these items should be reported in the cash flow statement when the instruments are redeemed in a manner consistent with interest costs (see para 6.29).

Example

A company issues a ten year zero coupon bond with a face value of £100,000 at a discount of £61,446. Its issue price is therefore £38,554 and the effective yield is 10%. How should the transaction be reflected in the cash flow statement?

At the issue date, the proceeds of £38,554 would be shown as a cash inflow in financing activity cash flows.

The discount of £61,446 represents a rolled-up interest charge which would be amortised to the income statement as a finance cost over the life of the bond while the bond remains outstanding. However, there would be no cash flow in these periods, because no cash has been paid.

On maturity, the question arises as to whether the repayment of £100,000 should be split between interest paid of £61,446 and repayment of long-term borrowings of £38,554. The alternative would be to classify the £100,000 as a repayment of long-term borrowing in the financing activity section of the cash flow statement.

The discount is in the nature of 'interest' which is part of finance costs in the income statement. Consequently, on maturity we recommend that the discount of £61,446 should be classified in the same manner as interest (see para 6.29) and disclosed as premium paid on redemption of bond. The balance of £38,554 should be classified as a financing activity cash flow as repayment of the bond.

A similar treatment would apply to the investor. The investor should record the payment for the bond of £38,554 as part of cash outflow in investing activities. On maturity, the receipt of £100,000 should be split classifying the £61,446 in the same manner as interest and the £38,554 as an investing activity cash flow.

11.5   Where debt instruments are redeemed at a premium, it will also be necessary to separate the principal and the interest element of the amounts paid on redemption. For example, where supplemental interest is paid on convertible bonds that are redeemed rather than converted, the whole amount of the supplemental interest accrued over the life of the bond and paid at redemption should be classified in the same manner as interest. Similar arguments would apply to non-equity shares that are redeemed at a premium.

Gains and losses

11.6   It is consistent with the objective of cash flow reporting that gains and losses that do not give rise to any cash flows should be excluded from the cash flow statement. Gains and losses are normally reported in the income statement or equity of the reporting entity. To the extent that these are included in arriving at net profit or loss, they should be adjusted (gains should be deducted and losses added) in the reconciliation to arrive at the net cash flow from operating activities when presented using the indirect method. For example, a gain on the sale of plant and machinery should be excluded from cash flow from operating activities. The gain is not a cash flow as such, but forms part of the proceeds from the sale that are disclosed under investing activities.

11.7   Similar treatment would apply to gains and losses on investments (other than cash equivalents). However, where investments are used for trading activities (typically by a bank or other financial institution), any gain or loss arising on their disposal during the year would be included in net profit. In this situation, net profit need only be adjusted for the movement in investments and not for the gain or loss arising (which is realised) to arrive at the net cash flow from operating activities. This is similar to the treatment of the movement in inventory.

11.8   In relation to debt securities, a further question arises as to whether a gain or loss that arises on the early settlement of a debt security issued by a reporting entity should be reported in the same manner as interest as it represents a change in the finance costs for the debt security, or as part of the capital repayment under financing activities. Consider the following example.

Example

The facts are the same as in the previous example (see para 35.166) except that the company has decided to redeem the bond early at the beginning of year 4 for £55,000.

The carrying value of the bond in the balance sheet at the end of year 3 is calculated as follows:

		£'000	£'000
Proceeds at the beginning of year 1			38,554
Interest accrued in year 1	10% on £38,554	3,855	
Interest accrued in year 2	10% on £42,408	4,241	
Interest accrued in year 3	10% on £46,649	4,665	
			12,761
Carrying value			
(capital value of bond £100,000 less unamortised			
discount of £61446 - £12761 = £48,685)			51,315
Loss on redemption:			
Redemption proceeds			55,000
Less carrying value			51,315
			3,685

The loss could be allocated to either:

- finance costs, giving £16,446 (£12,761 + £3,685) to be classified in the same manner as interest paid and £38,554 to be classified as a capital repayment under financing activity cash flows; or

- capital repayment, giving £42,239 (£38,554 + £3,685) to be reclassified as financing activity cash flows and £12,761 to be classified in the same manner as interest paid.

11.9 The first treatment should be used, because the total cash cost of the finance is then reflected in the cash flow statement. This is also consistent with the treatment of finance costs under IAS. The difference between the net proceeds of an instrument (in this example, £38,554) and the total amount of the payments made (£55,000) should be amortised to the income statement as finance cost (£16,446). The alternative of reporting the loss incurred as part of the capital repayment is not considered acceptable.

Reorganisation costs

11.10 Where a company undertakes to reorganise the business of an acquired subsidiary, it may incur costs that are provided for in periods prior to the actual disbursement of cash. The question arises as to whether the subsequent cash outflow in respect of the amount provided should be disclosed as part of the cash flows from operating or investing activities.

11.11 IAS 22, 'Business combinations', currently allows for such costs to be provided for as part of the fair value exercise on acquisition provided specific requirements are met. [IAS 22 para 31]. Otherwise, the provision should be recognised in the post-acquisition income statement of the acquiring group.

11.12 Where the requirements are not met, it is difficult to argue that the cash flows in respect of the reorganisation should be reported under investing activities as the provision has initially been recognised in the operating activities of the group. Such cash flows should be classified as operating cash flows.

11.13 Where the requirements are met the decision is not so clear cut. The provision has not been recognised in the income statement as an operating activity as it was recognised in the fair value exercise. This would support the argument for disclosing the cash flow as investing.

However, in order to treat all reorganisation costs consistently, we consider that the cash flows in relation to the provision recognised as part of the fair value exercise should be classified as an operating activity cash flow. In any case, such provisions will become rarer in future because in December 2002, the IASB issued an exposure draft (ED 3) on business combinations (phase 1) proposing that provisions for restructuring costs will only be permitted to be recognised in the fair value exercise if they are liabilities of the acquired entity at the date of acquisition.

Refinancing of borrowings

11.14 Companies may renegotiate their existing borrowings on terms that are different from those that were in place prior to the renegotiation. For example, as part of the renegotiation, a significant part of the company's current overdraft balance may be converted into a long-term loan. The question arises as to how such a reclassification should be dealt with in the cash flow statement.

11.15 The answer depends on whether the renegotiation gives rise to any cash flows. If the renegotiation is undertaken with the same bankers, it is likely that no cash flows are involved. In that situation, the proper treatment would be to reclassify the relevant portion of the overdraft balance in the cash and cash equivalents note with narrative disclosure of the transfer. On the other hand, if the refinancing is carried out with a different bank such that the proceeds of the new loan are utilised to settle all or part of the old overdraft balance, a cash inflow and outflow have taken place. Consequently, the new loan would be shown as a financing activity cash inflow with the result that the net movement in the overdraft balance will automatically be reflected in the increase or decrease in cash and cash equivalents during the year.

Cash subject to restriction

11.16 Sometimes cash may be held in a separate blocked account or an escrow account to be used only for a specific purpose, or held by subsidiaries operating in countries where exchange control restrictions are in force, such that cash is not freely transferable around the group. The question arises as to how restricted cash should be dealt with in the cash flow statement itself. Consider the following example.

Example

A property company secured development finance of £10m from its bankers during the year ended 31 December 20X1. The funds are held in a special blocked account to be used only for a specific development. Development on the property commenced during the year and by the end of its financial year the company expended £2m. At 31 December 20X1, there was a balance of £8m in the blocked account.

- There is a view that the balance of £8m in the blocked account should not be included in cash and cash equivalents, because to do so would create a distorted impression of the company's liquidity position. In that situation, the company would show the net cash outflow of £2m from operating activities, a cash inflow of £10m in financing with the balance of £8m as non-cash equivalent investments under investing activities. Adequate disclosure on the amount of and reason for the restrictions should be given in a note.

- An alternative treatment might be to treat the £8m balance as part of cash and cash equivalent with a clear explanation of the nature of the restriction given either on the face of the cash flow statement or in the note that reconciles the closing cash and cash equivalents for the cash flow statement with the balance sheet amounts.

On balance, the first treatment is preferable because it is difficult to argue in the second treatment that cash held in a special blocked deposit account would meet the definition of cash and cash equivalents.

11.17 In general, the treatment of cash subject to restriction should depend on the nature of the item and the restriction in force. Take the situation where a company is required to give a bond or a guarantee to a third party, for example, a bond may be held by Customs & Excise for the clearance of imported merchandise. In that situation, the payment to

Customs would form part of operating cash flows. Where there are restrictions on the transfer of cash and cash equivalents from a foreign subsidiary to the parent in the UK because of exchange control restrictions, the cash and cash equivalents balances held in the foreign subsidiary would be treated as part of group cash and cash equivalents in the cash flow statement, provided they meet the definition of cash and cash equivalents in the foreign subsidiary that owns them. This restriction would need to be disclosed. [IAS 7 para 48]. An example of disclosure is given in Table 10.

Table 10 – Disclosure of restricted cash balances included in cash and cash equivalents

Unaxis Holding AG – Annual Report – 31 December 2002

Note (13)

in CHF million

Cash and cash equivalents	**2002**	2001
Cash, postal and current bank accounts	**237**	274
Time deposits	**490**	576
Total	**726**	850
Change against previous year	**-124**	297
due to changes in Group companies	**-6**	-38
due to conversion differences	**-14**	-2

Some CHF 16 million of total cash and cash equivalents are located in countries in which certain forms or formal requests are required for the transfer of funds abroad. Nevertheless, if the Group complies with these requirements, such liquid funds are available at its disposition within a reasonable period.

Treatment of cash in the balance sheet

11.18 Cash and cash equivalents should be disclosed as a line item on the face of the balance sheet. [IAS 1 para 66(g)].

11.19 Cash should be recognised initially at the amount received by the entity or the amount received into the entity's bank account. Cash equivalents should initially be recognised at cost, which is the fair value of the consideration given to acquire the cash equivalent. [IAS 39 para 66]. Normally, no adjustment should be required to cash and cash equivalents balances except to update the exchange rate applied to balances denominated in foreign currencies and to reflect the effect of subsequent cash transactions.

Chapter 12

First-time adoption of IFRS

12.1 UK listed groups are required to apply EU-adopted international financial reporting standards in their consolidated financial statements for accounting periods beginning on or after 1 January 2005.

12.2 IFRS 1, 'First-time adoption of international financial reporting standards', was issued by the IASB in June 2003. This states that those companies adopting IFRS for the first time should apply those standards effective, with various exemptions available, at the reporting date of its first financial statements prepared under international financial reporting standards for the periods presented. Companies are required to apply IAS 7 in full.

12.3 As noted in paragraphs 2.3 and 2.4, the international standard is significantly different from the UK standard both in terms of the focus and presentation of cash flow information. In fact the international standard with its various options of presenting cash flows is much more flexible than the UK standard and, as a result, there is a diversity of presentations in practice. UK companies making the transition to international standards may find this confusing. It is quite likely that UK companies may begin a process of experimentation by retaining some of the features of FRS 1, such as voluntarily presenting a reconciliation to net debt as discussed in paragraph 10.7 above.

12.4 A significant difference between IAS 7 and FRS 1 is that IAS 7 uses three categories (operating, investing and financing activities) in its format, whereas FRS 1 uses nine. In addition, IAS 7 has more options for presentation than FRS 1. Another significant issue faced by UK companies on first-time adoption of IAS 7 will be the fact that IAS 7 requires the cash flow statement to reflect the movements in cash and cash equivalents, whereas FRS 1 requires the movements in cash only.

12.5 In addition, IAS 7 does not include the exemptions that are available under FRS 1. This should not affect listed companies which would have had to prepare cash flow statements anyway, but other companies that adopt IAS voluntarily after 2005 will have to prepare cash flow statements even if this was not previously required under UK GAAP.

Chapter 13

Worked example

13.1   A worked example showing how a cash flow statement would be prepared for a group in accordance with the standard is given below. In order to prepare a consolidated cash flow statement for Alphabeta Plc, the consolidated income statement, the consolidated balance sheet, the consolidated statement of changes in equity and certain other information related to the company are given. The starting point in the preparation of a cash flow statement is to compute all the increases and decreases in balance sheet amounts between the current period and the preceding period. Once the increases and decreases have been identified, each one must be analysed to determine its effect, if any, on the net cash provided or used in operating, investing or financing activities. If any increase or decrease affects more than one activity, each must be separately analysed. In the example, each figure in the cash flow statement can be traced to the income statement, statement of changes in equity or balance sheet (via workings) by following the letter references shown on the cash flow statement. The example does not deal with foreign currency operations as they have been covered in an earlier example (see para 9.10). Comparative figures for the cash flow statement have not been presented.

Example

Summarised below is the consolidated income statement and consolidated statement of changes in equity of Alphabeta Plc for the year ended 31 December 20X2, together with the (simplified) consolidated balance sheets as at 31 December 20X2 and 20X1. A cash flow statement for the group for the year ended 31 December 20X2 including notes to that statement is also given. The detailed workings supporting the figures in the cash flow statement follow immediately after the notes.

Alphabeta Plc
Consolidated income statement for the year ended 31 December 20X2

	£'000
Revenue	47,852
Cost of sales	(35,889)
Gross profit	11,963
Distribution costs	(2,814)
Administrative expenses	(5,250)
Other operating expenses	(17)
Profit from operations	3,882
Finance costs	(465)
Share of results of associates before tax	230
Investment income	126
Profit before tax	3,773
Taxation expense	(1,600)
Profit after tax	2,173
Minority interest	(425)
Net profit for the period	1,748

Alphabeta Plc
Consolidated statement of changes in equity for the year ended 31 December 20X2

	Share Capital £'000	Share Premium £'000	Other Reserves £'000	Accumulated profit £'000	Total £'000
Balance as at 1 January 20X2	12,000	600	392	3,260	16,252
Surplus on revaluation of properties	-	-	208	-	208
Net gains not recognised in the income statement	-	-	208	-	208
Net profit for the period	-	-	-	1,748	1,748
Dividends	-	-	-	(800)	(800)
Issue of share capital	600	400	-	-	1,000
Purchase of subsidiary	1,200	600	-	-	1,800
Share issue expenses	-	(75)	-	-	(75)
Balance as at 31 December 20X2	**13,800**	**1,525**	**600**	**4,208**	**20,133**

Alphabeta Plc
Consolidated balance sheet as at 31 December

	Notes	20X2 £'000	20X1 £'000
Assets			
Non-current assets			
Property plant and equipment	2	17,082	12,800
Goodwill	1	318	150
Patents and trade marks	1	80	50
Investments in associates	6	623	603
Available for sale investments	6	590	230
		18,693	13,833
Current assets			
Inventories	3	6,586	6,821
Trade and other receivables	4	7,327	4,415
Prepayments	4	648	375
Cash and cash equivalents		2,707	2,247
		17,268	13,858
Total assets		35,961	27,691
Shareholders' equity			
Share capital	8	13,800	12,000
Share premium	8	1,525	600
Other reserves		600	392
Retained earnings		4,208	3,260
		20,133	16,252
Minority interest	7	1,497	1,200
		21,630	17,452
Liabilities			
Non-current liabilities			
Long-term loans	9	1200	650
Retirement benefit obligations	10	426	103
Deferred tax liabilities	5	1182	725
Obligations under finance leases	5	614	676
		3,422	2,154
Current liabilities			
Bank overdrafts		1,014	700
Obligations under finance leases	5	245	174
Trade and other payables	5	6,004	4,353
Amounts owed to associate companies	5	193	243
Current tax liabilities	5	1,013	809
Accruals and other liabilities	5	1,640	1,106
Dividends payable	5	800	700
		10,909	8,085
Total equity and liabilities		35,961	27,691

Alphabeta Plc
Consolidated cash flow statement for the year ended
31 December 20X2

	Notes	£'000	£'000
Cash flows from operating activities			
Net profit		1,748	
Adjustments for			
Minority interest		425	
Tax charge		1,600	
Finance cost		465	
Investment income		(126)	
Share of results of associates before tax		(230)	
Fair value losses on available for sale investments	6a	17	
Depreciation	2a	1,345	
Amortisation of intangible fixed assets	1b	152	
Gain on sale of property, plant and equipment	2c	(45)	
		5,351	
Changes in working capital			
Decrease in inventories	3a	600	
Increase in trade and other receivables	4a	(2,432)	
Increase in prepayments	4b	(249)	
Increase in retirement benefit obligations	10a	323	
Increase in trade and other payables	5b	996	
Decrease in amounts owed to associates	5c	(50)	
Increase in accruals and other liabilities	5e	290	
Cash generated from operations		4,829	
Taxation paid	5d	(879)	
Premium paid on redemption of debentures	5g	(125)	
Interest paid	5f	(356)	
Net cash from operating activities			3,469
Cash flows from investing ivities			
Acquisition of subsidiary (net of cash acquired)	III	(115)	
Purchase of property, plant and equipment	2b	(3,974)	
Purchase of patents and trade marks	1a	(40)	
Proceeds from sale of property, plant and equipment	2d	503	
Purchase of available for sale investments	6b	(377)	
Dividends received	6c	150	
Interest received	4c	102	
Net cash used in investing activities			(3,751)

Cash flows from financing activities

Proceeds from issue of ordinary shares	**8b**	1,000
Share issue costs paid	**8a**	(75)
Repayment of debentures	**9b**	(200)
Proceeds from long-term borrowings	**9a**	750
Principal payments under finance lease	**5a**	(219)
Dividends paid to group shareholders	**5j**	(700)
Dividends paid to minority interests	**7a**	(128)
Net cash from financing activities		428
Increase in cash and cash equivalents		146
Cash and cash equivalents at the beginning of the year		1,547
Cash and cash equivalents at the end of the year	**II**	1,693

Alphabeta Plc
Notes to the cash flow statement

I. Accounting policy - Cash and cash equivalents

Cash and cash equivalents are carried in the balance sheet at cost. For the purposes of the cash flow statement, cash and cash equivalents comprise cash on hand, deposits held at call with banks, other short-term highly liquid investments with original maturities of three months or less and bank overdrafts.

II. Cash and cash equivalents

For the purposes of the cash flow statement, cash and cash equivalents comprise the following balance sheet amounts:

	£'000	**£'000**
Cash and cash equivalents	2,707	2,247
Bank overdrafts	(1,014)	(700)
	1,693	1,547

Included in cash and cash equivalents at the end of the period are £50,000 of deposits with banks held by a subsidiary that are restricted for use by the group due to foreign currency exchange restrictions.

III. Acquisition of subsidiary

On 1 March 20X2 a new wholly-owned subsidiary, Zeta Limited, was acquired by the issue of 1,200,000 ordinary shares of £1 each, whose fair market value was deemed to be £1.50 per share and £175,000 in cash. The fair values of Zeta Limited's identifiable assets and liabilities at the date of acquisition (including goodwill) were as follows:

The fair value of the assets and liabilities arising from the acquisition were:

Property, plant and equipment	1,550
Inventories	365
Trade and other receivables	480
Cash and bank balances	60
Trade and other payables	(655)
Accruals and other liabilities	(135)
	1,665
Goodwill	310
Total purchase consideration	1,975
Total purchase consideration	1,975
Less:	
Shares issued as consideration	(1,800)
Cash and bank balances in subsidiary acquired	(60)
Cash outflow on acquisition	115

IV. Major non-cash transactions

(i)   During the year the group entered into new finance lease arrangements in respect of equipment with a capital value at inception of the lease of £228,000.

(ii) A portion of the consideration for the purchase of the subsidiary Zeeta Limited in the period comprised shares. Further details of this acquisition set out in note III above.

Cash flow statement workings

1   Analysis of intangible fixed assets

		£'000	£'000
Net book value at 31 December 20X1			
Net book value of patents and trade marks		50	
Goodwill net of amortisation		150	
			200
Additions during the year			
Patents and trade marks	a	40	
Goodwill arising on acquisition of subsidiary		310	
			350
Amortisation for the year			
On patents		10	
On goodwill		142	
	b		(152)
Net book value at 31 December 20X2			398

2   Analysis of tangible fixed assets

		£'000
Net book value at 31 December 20X1		12,800
Addition in respect of new subsidiary		1,550
Additions		4,327
Surplus on revaluations		208
Net book value of disposals		(458)
Depreciation for the year	a	(1,345)
Net book value at 31 December 20X2		17,082

Additions during the year include a warehouse constructed by the group for £1,925,000 of which £125,000 related to interest capitalised and new equipment purchased on a finance lease with a fair value of £228,000. Included in administrative expenses is £45,000 for the gain arising on sale of fixed assets.

Additions as above		4,327
Less: leased assets		(228)
Less: capitalised interest (see workings note 5)		(125)
Cash paid	b	3,974
Net book value of disposals		458
Gain arising on sale	c	45
Proceeds of sale	d	503

Worked example

3   Stocks

	£'000
At 31 December 20X2	6,586
At 31 December 20X1	(6,821)
Decrease	(235)
Less: arising from acquisition of subsidiary	(365)
Net decrease included in reconciliation (note I) **a**	(600)

4   Analysis of debtors

Trade and other receivables
Trade debtors are stated net of provisions for bad debts of £960,000 in 20X2 and £485,000 in 20X1 respectively. The group wrote off £175,000 in bad debts and recognised an additional provision of £650,000 in administrative expenses.

Trade debtors	£'000
Trade debtors at 31 December 20X2	7,327
Trade debtors at 31 December 20X1	(4,415)
Increase	2,912
Less: arising on acquisition of subsidiary	(480)
Net increase included in reconciliation **a**	2,432

Note: The provision of £650,000 arising in the year has been included in the net movement on trade debtors and not separately identified.

Prepayments and accrued income
Included in prepayments and accrued income is interest receivable of £47,000 and £23,000 for 20X2 and 20X1 respectively.

	£'000	£'000
At 31 December 20X2	648	
Less: interest receivable	(47)	
		601
Less:		
At 31 December 20X1	375	
Less: interest receivable	(23)	(352)
Net increase included in reconciliation **b**		249

Interest received	£'000
Receivable at 31 December 20X1	23
Investment income per income statement	126
Receivable at 31 December 20X2	(47)
Cash received **c**	102

5 Analysis of creditors

Bank overdrafts for 20X2 and 20X1 are all repayable on demand and included in cash and cash equivalents.

Obligations under finance leases	£'000	£'000
Obligations at 31 December 20X1		
Less than one year	174	
More than one year	676	
		850
New capital lease		228
Obligations at 31 December 20X2		
Less than one year	245	
More than one year	614	(859)
Principal payment under finance leases a		219

Trade and other payables	£'000
At 31 December 20X2	6,004
At 31 December 20X1	(4,353)
Increase	1,651
Less: arising on acquisition of subsidiary	(655)
Net increase included in reconciliation b	996

Amounts owed to associated company	£'000
At 31 December 20X2	193
At 31 December 20X1	(243)
Net decrease c	(50)

Amounts owed to the associated company arise on trading activities

Taxation	£'000	£'000
Balance at 31 December 20X1		
Corporation tax	809	
Deferred tax	725	
		1,534
Tax charged per accounts:		
UK Corporation tax	980	
Transfer to deferred tax	457	
Prior year underprovision	103	
	1,540	1,540
Associated company	60	
Tax charged in income statement	1,600	
Balance at 31 December 20X2		
Corporation tax	1,013	
Deferred tax	1,182	(2,195)
Tax paid d		879

103

Accruals and other liabilities

Included in accruals at 31 December 20X2 and 20X1 is interest payable of £154,000
and £45,000 respectively.

		£'000	£'000
At 31 December 20X2		1,640	
Less: interest payable		(154)	
			1,486
Less:			
At 31 December 20X1		1,106	
Less: interest payable		(45)	(1,061)
Net increase			425
Less: arising on acquisition of subsidiary			(135)
Net increase included in reconciliation	e		290

Interest paid on loans and finance leases		£'000	£'000
Interest accrued at 31 December 20X1			45
Charge per income statement			
On overdrafts, bank and other loans		220	
On finance leases		120	
On premium paid on debenture redemption		125	465
Interest capitalised (see workings note 2)			125
Interest accrued at 31 December 20X2			(154)
Cash paid			481
Interest paid	f		356
Premium paid on debenture redemption	g		125
			481

Dividends paid by holding company		£'000
Balance at 31 December 20X1		700
Per statement of changes in equity		800
Balance at 31 December 20X2		(800)
Cash paid	j	700

6 Investments

		Associated company	Listed Investments
		£'000	£'000
Balance at 31 December 20X1		603	230
Share of retained profits		20	—
Decrease in fair value	a	—	(17)
Additions	b	—	377
Balance at 31 December 20X2		623	590
Share of associated company's profits (£230) less tax (£60)		170	
Less profits retained		20	
Dividends received	c	150	

Current asset investments
Current assets investments, which relate to British Government Securities, are classified as cash equivalents by the group.

7 Minority interests

		£'000
Balance at 31 December 20X1		1,200
Profit for the year		425
Balance at 31 December 20X2		(1,497)
Dividends paid to minority shareholders	a	128

8 Share capital and share premium

		£'000	£'000
At 31 December 20X2			
Share capital		13,800	
Share premium		1,525	15,325
At 31 December 20X1			
Share capital		12,000	
Share premium		600	(12,600)
Net increase			2,725
Less: issued for purchase of subsidiary			(1,800)
Add: share issue expenses written off	a		75
Balance issued for cash	b		1,000

9	**Debentures and other loans**		**£'000**
	At 31 December 20X2		1,200
	At 31 December 20X1		(650)
	Net increase		550
	Increase consists of:		
	New secured loans	**a**	750
	Repayment of debentures (nominal value)	**b**	(200)
			550

			£'000
10	**Retirement benefit obligations**		
	At 31 December 20X2		426
	At 31 December 20X1		
	Increase included in reconciliation		(103)
		a	323

Chapter 14

Comparison of IAS 7 and UK GAAP

14.1   The corresponding UK accounting standard is FRS 1, 'Cash flow statements'. A comparison of the rules in IAS 7 with UK GAAP is given in the table below. See also paragraph 10.9 onwards above for a discussion of the practical implications of the options for presentation in IAS 7.

IAS 7, Cash flow statements	FRS 1, Cash flow statements
Effective for accounting periods beginning on or after 1 January 1994.	*Effective for accounting periods ending on or after 23 March 1997.*
Related pronouncements	
-	-
Overview	
There are some major differences between a cash flow statement prepared under IAS 7 and one prepared under FRS 1. The cash flows reported under IAS 7 relate to movements in cash and cash equivalents (defined as short-term highly liquid investments that are readily convertible into known amounts of cash and subject to insignificant risk of changes in value). FRS 1 requires the movement of cash (defined as cash in hand and deposits repayable on demand, less overdrafts) to be reported in the cash flow statement. Under FRS 1, there is no concept of 'cash equivalents', but cash flows relating to IAS 7 'cash equivalents' would be included in 'management of liquid resources'. IAS 7 requires cash flows to be reported under three sections: operating, investing and financing, whereas FRS1 requires cash flows to be reported in far greater detail under nine standard headings. IAS 7 does not require a reconciliation of movements in cash flows to the movement in net debt. Under FRS 1, foreign currency exchange differences on cash balances are not reported on the face of the cash flow statement as they are non-cash items. However, IAS 7, requires foreign currency exchange differences on cash and cash equivalents to be reported on the face of the cash flow statement in order to reconcile the opening and closing cash and cash equivalent balances. IAS 7 has none of the exemptions that allow many entities not to prepare cash flow statements under FRS1.	
Convergence	
Not known at this stage, but the IASB is intending to reconsider IAS 7, as part of its work on the income statement.	

Summary of main points	
Scope	
Applies to all entities. [IAS 7 para 1].	Some entities are exempt including small entities and subsidiary undertakings where 90 per cent or more of the voting rights are controlled within the group, provided that the subsidiary is included in publicly available consolidated financial statements. [FRS 1 para 5].
Preparation	
The cash flow statement should include all the reporting entity's inflows and outflows of *cash and cash equivalents* for the period. [IAS 7 para 10, para 6].	The cash flow statement should include all the reporting entity's inflows and outflows of *cash* for the period. [FRS 1 para 6].
Cash comprises cash on hand and demand deposits. [IAS 7 para 6].	Similar. Cash is defined as cash in hand and deposits repayable on demand (that is, without notice and without penalty or if a period of notice is required it must not exceed 24 hours) with any qualifying financial institution, less overdrafts repayable on demand. [FRS 1 para 2].
Cash equivalents are short-term, highly liquid investments that are readily convertible to known amounts of cash and which are subject to an insignificant risk of changes in value. [IAS 7 para 7].	No concept of 'cash equivalents', but cash flows relating to IAS 7 'cash equivalents' are reported under the heading 'Management of liquid resources'.
-	Liquid resources are current asset investments that are readily disposable (that is, disposable by the reporting entity without curtailing or disrupting its business; and either readily convertible into known amounts of cash at or close to carrying amount, or traded in an active market). [FRS 1 para 2].
Format	
Cash flows should be classified under the following standard headings. [IAS 7 para 10] :	Cash flows should be classified under the following standard headings. [FRS 1 para 7]:
• Operating activities. (Includes principal revenue-producing activities and other activities that are not investing or financing.) [IAS 7 para 6].	• Operating activities. • Dividends from joint ventures and associates. • Returns on investments and servicing of finance.
• Investing activities. (Includes acquisition and disposal of long-term assets and other investments not included in cash equivalents.) [IAS 7 para 6].	• Taxation • Capital expenditure and financial investments. • Acquisitions and disposals.

• Financing activities. (Includes activities that result in changes in the size and composition of the equity capital and borrowings.) [IAS 7 para 6].	• Equity dividends paid. • Management of liquid resources. • Financing.
Individual categories of cash inflows and outflows must be shown under the appropriate headings on the face of the primary cash flow statement. [IAS 7 para 21].	Individual categories can be shown in the notes and so the primary cash flow statement can include only the cash flows relating to the standard headings shown above. [FRS 1 para 8].

Classification

No separate heading.	Dividends received from joint ventures and associates should be included as separate items between operating activities and returns on investment and servicing of finance. [FRS 1 para 12A].
Interest paid or interest and dividends received may be classified as operating, investing or financing activities. [IAS 7 para 31].	Separate heading 'Returns on investments and servicing of finance' includes receipts from investments and payments to providers of finance, non-equity shareholders and minority interests. [FRS 1 para13].
Dividends paid may be classified as operating or financing cash flows. [IAS 7 para 34].	Separate heading for equity dividends paid. [FRS 1 para 7].
Tax cash flows should be included under operating activities, unless they can be specifically identified with a financing or investing activity in which case they should be reported under those headings as appropriate [IAS 7 para 35] with disclosure of total tax paid [IAS 7 para 36].	'Taxation' includes cash flows to or from taxation authorities in respect of the reporting entity's revenue and capital profits. [FRS 1 para 16].
Extraordinary items are classified under the relevant headings according to their nature. [IAS 7 para 29].	Exceptional and extraordinary items are classified under the relevant headings according to their nature. [FRS 1 para 37]. Also disclose exceptional cash flows where no exceptional item is reported in the profit and loss account. [FRS 1 para 38].

Gross or net cash flows	
Report gross inflows and outflows [IAS 7 para 18, para21], except for:	Report gross inflows and outflows [FRS 1 para 8], except for:
Cash flows from operating activities can be reported net under the indirect method. [IAS 7 para 18(b)].	Same. [FRS 1 para 7].
Cash receipts and payments on behalf of customers when the cash flows reflect the activities of the customer rather than the entity. [IAS 7 para22(a)].	No equivalent provision.
Cash receipts and payments may be reported net for items for which the turnover is quick, the amounts are large and the maturities are short. [IAS 7 para 22(b)].	Similar. Cash inflows and outflows may be reported net for items with short maturities and high turnover occurring from rollover or reissue; or a single financing transaction (which fulfils all the conditions of FRS 4 para 35). [FRS 1 para 9].
Foreign currency	
Exchange differences on cash and cash equivalents are reported on the face of primary cash flow statement in order to reconcile opening and closing cash and cash equivalent balances. [IAS 7 para 28].	Exchange differences on cash are non-cash items and are not reported on the face of the primary cash flow statement.
The reporting entity's own foreign currency cash flows should be translated at the exchange rate at the dates of the cash flows (or a weighted average exchange rate for the period). [IAS 7 para 25].	Similar treatment.
The cash flows of a foreign subsidiary should be translated at the exchange at the dates of the cash flows (or a weighted average exchange rate for the period). [IAS 7 para 26].	The cash flows of a foreign subsidiary should be translated on the basis used for translating the results in the consolidated profit and loss account (that is average or closing rate). The actual rate at the date of the transaction can be used for intra-group transactions. [FRS 1 para 41].
Acquisitions and disposals	
Cash paid or received as purchase or sale consideration is reported in the cash flow statement net of cash and cash equivalents acquired or disposed of (under investing activities). [IAS 7 para 42].	Cash paid or received as purchase or sale consideration is disclosed separately from cash balances acquired or disposed of (under acquisition and disposals). [FRS 1 paras 23, 24].
Disclose summary of the effects of acquisitions and disposals of subsidiary undertakings (and other businesses) indicating how much of the consideration comprised *cash and cash equivalents*. [IAS 7 para 40].	Disclose summary of the effects of acquisitions and disposals of subsidiary undertakings (and other businesses) indicating how much of the consideration comprised *cash*. [FRS 1 para 45].
Disclose net cash flows attributable to operating, investing and financing activities of discontinuing operations. [IAS 35 para 27(g)].	Disclose the effects of acquisitions and disposals on amounts reported under each of the standard headings. [FRS 1 para 45].

Other notes to the cash flow statements	
Reconciliation of net profit to net cash flow reported on the face of the cash flow statement or in the notes. [IAS 7 para 20].	Reconciliation of net operating profit to net cash flow reported as a separate statement. [FRS 1 para 12].
No equivalent requirement.	Reconciliation to net debt. [FRS 1 para 33].
Components of cash and cash equivalents and reconciliation to amounts presented in the balance sheet. [IAS 7 para 45].	Analysis of changes in net debt and reconciliation to amounts presented in the balance sheet. [FRS 1 para 33].
Non cash transactions. [IAS 7 para 43].	Non cash transactions. [FRS 1 para 46].
Restricted cash balances – disclose, together with a commentary, significant cash and cash equivalent balances held by the entity that are not available for use by the group. [IAS 7 para 48].	Restriction on remittability – identify amounts and explain circumstances that prevent the transfer of cash from one part of the group to another. [FRS 1 para 47].
IAS 35 requires separate disclosure of the cash flow activity of discontinuing operations for the period. [IAS 35 para 27(g)].	Disclosure of cash flows from discontinued operations is encouraged. [FRS 1 para 56].
Disclosure encouraged	
Reporting of gross operating cash flows. [IAS 7 para 19].	Reporting of gross operating cash flows. [FRS 1 para 7].
Unused borrowing facilities. [IAS 7 para 50(a)].	Listed companies are required to give an analysis of the maturity of any material undrawn committed borrowing facilities. [FRS 13 para 40].
Aggregate amounts of each of the operating, investing and financing cash flows related to interests in joint ventures reported using proportional consolidation. [IAS 7 para 50(b)].	No equivalent disclosure as proportional consolidation is not permitted under UK GAAP.
Operating capacity – separate disclosure of cash flows representing increases in operating capacity from those required to maintain operating capacity. [IAS 7 para 50(c)].	The statement on the operating and financial review encourages disclosure of investment for the future. [OFR para 23].
Segmental cash flows – operating, investing and financing cash flows for each reported industry and geographical segments. [IAS 7 para 50(d)].	Segmental cash flow information [FRS 1 para 8] - also encouraged by statement on the operating and financial review [OFR para 33].

Appendix

IAS 7 Cash Flow Statements

This Standard became effective for financial statements covering periods beginning on or after 1 January 1994.

Contents

APPENDICES

IAS 7 International Accounting Standard

Cash Flow Statements

International Accounting Standard 7 *Cash Flow Statements* (IAS 7) is set out in paragraphs 1-53. All the paragraphs have equal authority but retain the IASC format of the Standard when it was adopted by the IASB. The scope and authority of IASs are explained in the *Preface to International Financial Reporting Standards*. IAS 7 is accompanied by application guidance, as set out in Appendices A and B. IAS 7 should be read in the context of its objective and the *Framework for the Preparation and Presentation of Financial Statements*, which provide a basis for selecting and applying accounting policies in the absence of explicit guidance.

Objective

Information about the cash flows of an enterprise is useful in providing users of financial statements with a basis to assess the ability of the enterprise to generate cash and cash equivalents and the needs of the enterprise to utilise those cash flows. The economic decisions that are taken by users require an evaluation of the ability of an enterprise to generate cash and cash equivalents and the timing and certainty of their generation.

The objective of this Standard is to require the provision of information about the historical changes in cash and cash equivalents of an enterprise by means of a cash flow statement which classifies cash flows during the period from operating, investing and financing activities.

Scope

1. *An enterprise should prepare a cash flow statement in accordance with the requirements of this Standard and should present it as an integral part of its financial statements for each period for which financial statements are presented.*

2. This Standard supersedes IAS 7 *Statement of Changes in Financial Position*, approved in July 1977.

3. Users of an enterprise's financial statements are interested in how the enterprise generates and uses cash and cash equivalents. This is the case regardless of the nature of the enterprise's activities and irrespective of whether cash can be viewed as the product of the enterprise, as may be the case with a financial institution. Enterprises need cash for essentially the same reasons however different their principal revenue-producing activities might be. They need cash to conduct their operations, to pay their obligations, and to provide returns to their investors. Accordingly, this Standard requires all enterprises to present a cash flow statement.

Benefits of Cash Flow Information

4. A cash flow statement, when used in conjunction with the rest of the financial statements, provides information that enables users to evaluate the changes in net assets of an enterprise, its financial structure (including its liquidity and solvency) and its ability to affect the amounts and timing of cash flows in order to adapt to changing circumstances and opportunities. Cash flow information is useful in assessing the ability of the enterprise to generate cash and cash equivalents and enables users to develop models to assess and compare the present value of the future cash flows of different enterprises. It also enhances the comparability of the reporting of operating performance by different enterprises because it eliminates the effects of using different accounting treatments for the same transactions and events.

5.   Historical cash flow information is often used as an indicator of the amount, timing and certainty of future cash flows. It is also useful in checking the accuracy of past assessments of future cash flows and in examining the relationship between profitability and net cash flow and the impact of changing prices.

Definitions

6.   *The following terms are used in this Standard with the meanings specified:*

Cash comprises cash on hand and demand deposits.

Cash equivalents are short-term, highly liquid investments that are readily convertible to known amounts of cash and which are subject to an insignificant risk of changes in value.

Cash flows are inflows and outflows of cash and cash equivalents.

Operating activities are the principal revenue-producing activities of the enterprise and other activities that are not investing or financing activities.

Investing activities are the acquisition and disposal of long-term assets and other investments not included in cash equivalents.

Financing activities are activities that result in changes in the size and composition of the equity capital and borrowings of the enterprise.

Cash and Cash Equivalents

7.   Cash equivalents are held for the purpose of meeting short-term cash commitments rather than for investment or other purposes. For an investment to qualify as a cash equivalent it must be readily convertible to a known amount of cash and be subject to an

insignificant risk of changes in value. Therefore, an investment normally qualifies as a cash equivalent only when it has a short maturity of, say, three months or less from the date of acquisition. Equity investments are excluded from cash equivalents unless they are, in substance, cash equivalents, for example in the case of preferred shares acquired within a short period of their maturity and with a specified redemption date.

8. Bank borrowings are generally considered to be financing activities. However, in some countries, bank overdrafts which are repayable on demand form an integral part of an enterprise's cash management. In these circumstances, bank overdrafts are included as a component of cash and cash equivalents. A characteristic of such banking arrangements is that the bank balance often fluctuates from being positive to overdrawn.

9. Cash flows exclude movements between items that constitute cash or cash equivalents because these components are part of the cash management of an enterprise rather than part of its operating, investing and financing activities. Cash management includes the investment of excess cash in cash equivalents.

Presentation of a Cash Flow Statement

10. *The cash flow statement should report cash flows during the period classified by operating, investing and financing activities.*

11. An enterprise presents its cash flows from operating, investing and financing activities in a manner which is most appropriate to its business. Classification by activity provides information that allows users to assess the impact of those activities on the financial position of the enterprise and the amount of its cash and cash equivalents. This information may also be used to evaluate the relationships among those activities.

12. A single transaction may include cash flows that are classified differently. For example, when the cash repayment of a loan

includes both interest and capital, the interest element may be classified as an operating activity and the capital element is classified as a financing activity.

Operating Activities

13. The amount of cash flows arising from operating activities is a key indicator of the extent to which the operations of the enterprise have generated sufficient cash flows to repay loans, maintain the operating capability of the enterprise, pay dividends and make new investments without recourse to external sources of financing. Information about the specific components of historical operating cash flows is useful, in conjunction with other information, in forecasting future operating cash flows.

14. Cash flows from operating activities are primarily derived from the principal revenue-producing activities of the enterprise. Therefore, they generally result from the transactions and other events that enter into the determination of net profit or loss. Examples of cash flows from operating activities are:

(a) cash receipts from the sale of goods and the rendering of services;

(b) cash receipts from royalties, fees, commissions and other revenue;

(c) cash payments to suppliers for goods and services;

(d) cash payments to and on behalf of employees;

(e) cash receipts and cash payments of an insurance enterprise for premiums and claims, annuities and other policy benefits;

(f)   cash payments or refunds of income taxes unless they can be specifically identified with financing and investing activities; and

(g)   cash receipts and payments from contracts held for dealing or trading purposes.

Some transactions, such as the sale of an item of plant, may give rise to a gain or loss which is included in the determination of net profit or loss. However, the cash flows relating to such transactions are cash flows from investing activities.

15.   An enterprise may hold securities and loans for dealing or trading purposes, in which case they are similar to inventory acquired specifically for resale. Therefore, cash flows arising from the purchase and sale of dealing or trading securities are classified as operating activities. Similarly, cash advances and loans made by financial institutions are usually classified as operating activities since they relate to the main revenue-producing activity of that enterprise.

Investing Activities

16.   The separate disclosure of cash flows arising from investing activities is important because the cash flows represent the extent to which expenditures have been made for resources intended to generate future income and cash flows. Examples of cash flows arising from investing activities are:

(a)   cash payments to acquire property, plant and equipment, intangibles and other long-term assets. These payments include those relating to capitalised development costs and self-constructed property, plant and equipment;

(b)   cash receipts from sales of property, plant and equipment, intangibles and other long-term assets;

(c) cash payments to acquire equity or debt instruments of other enterprises and interests in joint ventures (other than payments for those instruments considered to be cash equivalents or those held for dealing or trading purposes);

(d) cash receipts from sales of equity or debt instruments of other enterprises and interests in joint ventures (other than receipts for those instruments considered to be cash equivalents and those held for dealing or trading purposes);

(e) cash advances and loans made to other parties (other than advances and loans made by a financial institution);

(f) cash receipts from the repayment of advances and loans made to other parties (other than advances and loans of a financial institution);

(g) cash payments for futures contracts, forward contracts, option contracts and swap contracts except when the contracts are held for dealing or trading purposes, or the payments are classified as financing activities; and

(h) cash receipts from futures contracts, forward contracts, option contracts and swap contracts except when the contracts are held for dealing or trading purposes, or the receipts are classified as financing activities.
When a contract is accounted for as a hedge of an identifiable position, the cash flows of the contract are classified in the same manner as the cash flows of the position being hedged.

Financing Activities

17. The separate disclosure of cash flows arising from financing activities is important because it is useful in predicting claims on future cash flows by providers of capital to the enterprise. Examples of cash flows arising from financing activities are:

    (a)   cash proceeds from issuing shares or other equity instruments;

    (b)   cash payments to owners to acquire or redeem the enterprise's shares;

    (c)   cash proceeds from issuing debentures, loans, notes, bonds, mortgages and other short or long-term borrowings;

    (d)   cash repayments of amounts borrowed; and

    (e)   cash payments by a lessee for the reduction of the outstanding liability relating to a finance lease.

Reporting Cash Flows from Operating Activities

18.   *An enterprise should report cash flows from operating activities using either:*

    (a)   the direct method, whereby major classes of gross cash receipts and gross cash payments are disclosed; or

    (b)   the indirect method, whereby net profit or loss is adjusted for the effects of transactions of a non-cash nature, any deferrals or accruals of past or future operating cash receipts or payments, and items of income or expense associated with investing or financing cash flows.

19.   Enterprises are encouraged to report cash flows from operating activities using the direct method. The direct method provides information which may be useful in estimating future cash flows and which is not available under the indirect method. Under the direct method, information about major classes of gross cash receipts and gross cash payments may be obtained either:

    (a)   from the accounting records of the enterprise; or

(b)   by adjusting sales, cost of sales (interest and similar income and interest expense and similar charges for a financial institution) and other items in the income statement for:

(i)   changes during the period in inventories and operating receivables and payables;

(ii)   other non-cash items; and

(iii)   other items for which the cash effects are investing or financing cash flows.

20.   Under the indirect method, the net cash flow from operating activities is determined by adjusting net profit or loss for the effects of:

(a)   changes during the period in inventories and operating receivables and payables;

(b)   non-cash items such as depreciation, provisions, deferred taxes, unrealised foreign currency gains and losses, undistributed profits of associates, and minority interests; and

(c)   all other items for which the cash effects are investing or financing cash flows.
        Alternatively, the net cash flow from operating activities may be presented under the indirect method by showing the revenues and expenses disclosed in the income statement and the changes during the period in inventories and operating receivables and payables.

Reporting Cash Flows from Investing and Financing Activities

21.   *An enterprise should report separately major classes of gross cash receipts and gross cash payments arising from investing*

and financing activities, except to the extent that cash flows described in paragraphs 22 and 24 are reported on a net basis.

Reporting Cash Flows on a Net Basis

22. *Cash flows arising from the following operating, investing or financing activities may be reported on a net basis:*

    (a) *cash receipts and payments on behalf of customers when the cash flows reflect the activities of the customer rather than those of the enterprise; and*

    (b) *cash receipts and payments for items in which the turnover is quick, the amounts are large, and the maturities are short.*

23. Examples of cash receipts and payments referred to in paragraph 22(a) are:

    (a) the acceptance and repayment of demand deposits of a bank;

    (b) funds held for customers by an investment enterprise; and

    (c) rents collected on behalf of, and paid over to, the owners of properties.

    Examples of cash receipts and payments referred to in paragraph 22(b) are advances made for, and the repayment of:

    (a) principal amounts relating to credit card customers;

    (b) the purchase and sale of investments; and

    (c) other short-term borrowings, for example, those which have a maturity period of three months or less.

24. *Cash flows arising from each of the following activities of a financial institution may be reported on a net basis:*

    (a)   *cash receipts and payments for the acceptance and repayment of deposits with a fixed maturity date;*

    (b)   *the placement of deposits with and withdrawal of deposits from other financial institutions; and*

    (c)   *cash advances and loans made to customers and the repayment of those advances and loans.*

Foreign Currency Cash Flows

25. *Cash flows arising from transactions in a foreign currency should be recorded in an enterprise's reporting currency by applying to the foreign currency amount the exchange rate between the reporting currency and the foreign currency at the date of the cash flow.*

26. *The cash flows of a foreign subsidiary should be translated at the exchange rates between the reporting currency and the foreign currency at the dates of the cash flows.*

27. Cash flows denominated in a foreign currency are reported in a manner consistent with IAS 21 *Accounting for the Effects of Changes in Foreign Exchange Rates*. This permits the use of an exchange rate that approximates the actual rate. For example, a weighted average exchange rate for a period may be used for recording foreign currency transactions or the translation of the cash flows of a foreign subsidiary. However, IAS 21 does not permit use of the exchange rate at the balance sheet date when translating the cash flows of a foreign subsidiary.

28. Unrealised gains and losses arising from changes in foreign currency exchange rates are not cash flows. However, the effect of exchange rate changes on cash and cash equivalents held or due in

a foreign currency is reported in the cash flow statement in order to reconcile cash and cash equivalents at the beginning and the end of the period. This amount is presented separately from cash flows from operating, investing and financing activities and includes the differences, if any, had those cash flows been reported at end of period exchange rates.

Extraordinary Items

29. *The cash flows associated with extraordinary items should be classified as arising from operating, investing or financing activities as appropriate and separately disclosed.*

30. The cash flows associated with extraordinary items are disclosed separately as arising from operating, investing or financing activities in the cash flow statement, to enable users to understand their nature and effect on the present and future cash flows of the enterprise. These disclosures are in addition to the separate disclosures of the nature and amount of extraordinary items required by IAS 8 *Net Profit or Loss for the Period, Fundamental Errors and Changes in Accounting Policies.*

Interest and Dividends

31. *Cash flows from interest and dividends received and paid should each be disclosed separately. Each should be classified in a consistent manner from period to period as either operating, investing or financing activities.*

32. The total amount of interest paid during a period is disclosed in the cash flow statement whether it has been recognised as an expense in the income statement or capitalised in accordance with the allowed alternative treatment in IAS 23 *Borrowing Costs.*

33. Interest paid and interest and dividends received are usually classified as operating cash flows for a financial institution.

However, there is no consensus on the classification of these cash flows for other enterprises. Interest paid and interest and dividends received may be classified as operating cash flows because they enter into the determination of net profit or loss. Alternatively, interest paid and interest and dividends received may be classified as financing cash flows and investing cash flows respectively, because they are costs of obtaining financial resources or returns on investments.

34. Dividends paid may be classified as a financing cash flow because they are a cost of obtaining financial resources. Alternatively, dividends paid may be classified as a component of cash flows from operating activities in order to assist users to determine the ability of an enterprise to pay dividends out of operating cash flows.

Taxes on Income

35. *Cash flows arising from taxes on income should be separately disclosed and should be classified as cash flows from operating activities unless they can be specifically identified with financing and investing activities.*

36. Taxes on income arise on transactions that give rise to cash flows that are classified as operating, investing or financing activities in a cash flow statement. While tax expense may be readily identifiable with investing or financing activities, the related tax cash flows are often impracticable to identify and may arise in a different period from the cash flows of the underlying transaction. Therefore, taxes paid are usually classified as cash flows from operating activities. However, when it is practicable to identify the tax cash flow with an individual transaction that gives rise to cash flows that are classified as investing or financing activities the tax cash flow is classified as an investing or financing activity as appropriate. When tax cash flows are allocated over more than one class of activity, the total amount of taxes paid is disclosed.

Investments in Subsidiaries, Associates and Joint Ventures

37. When accounting for an investment in an associate or a subsidiary accounted for by use of the equity or cost method, an investor restricts its reporting in the cash flow statement to the cash flows between itself and the investee, for example, to dividends and advances.

38. An enterprise which reports its interest in a jointly controlled entity (see IAS 31 *Financial Reporting of Interests in Joint Ventures*) using proportionate consolidation, includes in its consolidated cash flow statement its proportionate share of the jointly controlled entity's cash flows. An enterprise which reports such an interest using the equity method includes in its cash flow statement the cash flows in respect of its investments in the jointly controlled entity, and distributions and other payments or receipts between it and the jointly controlled entity.

Acquisitions and Disposals of Subsidiaries and Other Business Units

39. *The aggregate cash flows arising from acquisitions and from disposals of subsidiaries or other business units should be presented separately and classified as investing activities.*

40. *An enterprise should disclose, in aggregate, in respect of both acquisitions and disposals of subsidiaries or other business units during the period each of the following:*

    (a)   the total purchase or disposal consideration;

    (b)   the portion of the purchase or disposal consideration discharged by means of cash and cash equivalents;

    (c)   the amount of cash and cash equivalents in the subsidiary or business unit acquired or disposed of; and

(d)   *the amount of the assets and liabilities other than cash or cash equivalents in the subsidiary or business unit acquired or disposed of, summarised by each major category.*

41.   The separate presentation of the cash flow effects of acquisitions and disposals of subsidiaries and other business units as single line items, together with the separate disclosure of the amounts of assets and liabilities acquired or disposed of, helps to distinguish those cash flows from the cash flows arising from the other operating, investing and financing activities. The cash flow effects of disposals are not deducted from those of acquisitions.

42.   The aggregate amount of the cash paid or received as purchase or sale consideration is reported in the cash flow statement net of cash and cash equivalents acquired or disposed of.

Non-cash Transactions

43.   *Investing and financing transactions that do not require the use of cash or cash equivalents should be excluded from a cash flow statement. Such transactions should be disclosed elsewhere in the financial statements in a way that provides all the relevant information about these investing and financing activities.*

44.   Many investing and financing activities do not have a direct impact on current cash flows although they do affect the capital and asset structure of an enterprise. The exclusion of non-cash transactions from the cash flow statement is consistent with the objective of a cash flow statement as these items do not involve cash flows in the current period. Examples of non-cash transactions are:

(a)   the acquisition of assets either by assuming directly related liabilities or by means of a finance lease;

(b)   the acquisition of an enterprise by means of an equity issue; and

(c)   the conversion of debt to equity.

Components of Cash and Cash Equivalents

45.   *An enterprise should disclose the components of cash and cash equivalents and should present a reconciliation of the amounts in its cash flow statement with the equivalent items reported in the balance sheet.*

46.   In view of the variety of cash management practices and banking arrangements around the world and in order to comply with IAS 1 *Presentation of Financial Statements*, an enterprise discloses the policy which it adopts in determining the composition of cash and cash equivalents.

47.   The effect of any change in the policy for determining components of cash and cash equivalents, for example, a change in the classification of financial instruments previously considered to be part of an enterprise's investment portfolio, is reported in accordance with IAS 8 *Net Profit or Loss for the Period, Fundamental Errors and Changes in Accounting Policies.*

Other Disclosures

48.   *An enterprise should disclose, together with a commentary by management, the amount of significant cash and cash equivalent balances held by the enterprise that are not available for use by the group.*

49.   There are various circumstances in which cash and cash equivalent balances held by an enterprise are not available for use by the group. Examples include cash and cash equivalent balances held by a subsidiary that operates in a country where exchange

controls or other legal restrictions apply when the balances are not available for general use by the parent or other subsidiaries.

50. Additional information may be relevant to users in understanding the financial position and liquidity of an enterprise. Disclosure of this information, together with a commentary by management, is encouraged and may include:

(a) the amount of undrawn borrowing facilities that may be available for future operating activities and to settle capital commitments, indicating any restrictions on the use of these facilities;

(b) the aggregate amounts of the cash flows from each of operating, investing and financing activities related to interests in joint ventures reported using proportionate consolidation;

(c) the aggregate amount of cash flows that represent increases in operating capacity separately from those cash flows that are required to maintain operating capacity; and

(d) the amount of the cash flows arising from the operating, investing and financing activities of each reported industry and geographical segment (see IAS 14 *Segment Reporting*).

51. The separate disclosure of cash flows that represent increases in operating capacity and cash flows that are required to maintain operating capacity is useful in enabling the user to determine whether the enterprise is investing adequately in the maintenance of its operating capacity. An enterprise that does not invest adequately in the maintenance of its operating capacity may be prejudicing future profitability for the sake of current liquidity and distributions to owners.

52.   The disclosure of segmental cash flows enables users to obtain a better understanding of the relationship between the cash flows of the business as a whole and those of its component parts and the availability and variability of segmental cash flows.

Effective Date

53.   *This International Accounting Standard becomes operative for financial statements covering periods beginning on or after 1 January 1994.*

Appendix A

Cash Flow Statement for an Enterprise other than a Financial Institution

The appendix is illustrative only and does not form part of the Standard. The purpose of the appendix is to illustrate the application of the Standard to assist in clarifying its meaning.

1. The examples show only current period amounts. Corresponding amounts for the preceding period are required to be presented in accordance with IAS 1 *Presentation of Financial Statements.*

2. Information from the income statement and balance sheet is provided to show how the statements of cash flows under the direct method and indirect method have been derived. Neither the income statement nor the balance sheet are presented in conformity with the disclosure and presentation requirements of International Accounting Standards.

3. The following additional information is also relevant for the preparation of the statements of cash flows:

    •   all of the shares of a subsidiary were acquired for 590. The fair values of assets acquired and liabilities assumed were as follows:

Inventories	100
Accounts receivable	100
Cash	40
Property, plant and equipment	650
Trade payables	100
Long-term debt	200

    •   250 was raised from the issue of share capital and a further 250 was raised from long-term borrowings.

- interest expense was 400 of which 170 was paid during the period. 100 relating to interest expense of the prior period was also paid during the period.

- dividends paid were 1,200.

- the liability for tax at the beginning and end of the period was 1,000 and 400 respectively. During the period, a further 200 tax was provided for. Withholding tax on dividends received amounted to 100.

- during the period, the group acquired property, plant and equipment with an aggregate cost of 1,250 of which 900 was acquired by means of finance leases. Cash payments of 350 were made to purchase property, plant and equipment.

- plant with original cost of 80 and accumulated depreciation of 60 was sold for 20.

- accounts receivable as at end of 19-2 include 100 of interest receivable.

Consolidated Income Statement for the period ended 19-2

Sales	30,650
Cost of sales	(26,000)
Gross profit	4,650
Depreciation	(450)
Administrative and selling expenses	(910)
Interest expense	(400)
Investment income	500
Foreign exchange loss	(40)
Net profit before taxation and extraordinary item	3,350
Extraordinary item - Insurance proceeds from earthquake disaster settlement	180
Net profit after extraordinary item	3,530
Taxes on income	(300)
Net profit	3,230

Consolidated Balance Sheet as at end of 19-2

		19-2		19-1
Assets				
Cash and cash equivalents		410		160
Accounts receivable		1,900		1,200
Inventory		1,000		1,950
Portfolio investments		2,500		2,500
Property, plant and equipment at cost	3,730		1,910	
Accumulated depreciation	(1,450)		(1,060)	
Property, plant and equipment net		2,280		850
Total assets		8,090		6,660
Liabilities				
Trade payables		250		1,890
Interest payable		230		100
Income taxes payable		400		1,000
Long term debt		2,300		1,040
Total liabilities		3,180		4,030
Shareholders' Equity				
Share capital		1,500		1,250
Retained earnings		3,410		1,380
Total shareholders equity		4,910		2,630
Total liabilities and shareholders equity		8,090		6,660

Direct Method Cash Flow Statement (paragraph 18a)

		19-2
Cash flows from operating activities		
Cash receipts from customers	30,150	
Cash paid to suppliers and employees	(27,600)	
Cash generated from operations	2,550	
Interest paid	(270)	
Income taxes paid	(900)	
Cash flow before extraordinary item	1,380	
Proceeds from earthquake disaster settlement	180	
Net cash from operating activities		1,560

Cash flows from investing activities

Acquisition of subsidiary X, net of cash acquired (Note A)	(550)	
Purchase of property, plant and equipment (Note B)	(350)	
Proceeds from sale of equipment	20	
Interest received	200	
Dividends received	200	
Net cash used in investing activities		(480)

Cash flows from financing activities

Proceeds from issuance of share capital	250	
Proceeds from long-term borrowings	250	
Payment of finance lease liabilities	(90)	
Dividends paid*	(1,200)	
Net cash used in financing activities		(790)
Net increase in cash and cash equivalents		290
Cash and cash equivalents at beginning of period (note C)		120
Cash and cash equivalents at end of period (note C)		410

---

*This could also be shown as an operating cash flow.

Indirect Method Cash Flow Statement (paragraph 18b)

19-2

Cash flows from operating activities

Net profit before taxation, and extraordinary item.	3,350	
Adjustments for:		
Depreciation	450	
Foreign exchange loss	40	
Investment income	(500)	
Interest expense	400	
	3,740	
Increase in trade and other receivables	(500)	
Decrease in inventories	1,050	
Decrease in trade payables	(1,740)	
Cash generated from operations	2,550	
Interest paid	(270)	
Income taxes paid	(900)	
Cash flow before extraordinary item	1,380	
Proceeds from earthquake disaster settlement	180	
Net cash from operating activities		1,560

Cash flows from investing activities

Acquisition of subsidiary X net of cash acquired (Note A)	(550)	
Purchase of property, plant and equipment (Note B)	(350)	
Proceeds from sale of equipment	20	
Interest received	200	
Dividends received	200	
Net cash used in investing activities		(480)

Cash flows from financing activities

Proceeds from issuance of share capital	250	
Proceeds from long-term borrowings	250	
Payment of finance lease liabilities	(90)	
Dividends paid*	(1,200)	
Net cash used in financing activities		(790)
Net increase in cash and cash equivalents		290
Cash and cash equivalents at beginning of period (Note C)		120
Cash and cash equivalents at end of period(Note C)		410

---

*This could also be shown as an operating cash flow.

Notes to the Cash Flow Statement
(direct method and indirect method)

A. Acquisition of Subsidiary

During the period the group acquired subsidiary X. The fair value of assets acquired and liabilities assumed were as follows:

Cash	40
Inventories	100
Accounts receivable	100
Property, plant and equipment	650
Trade payables	(100)
Long-term debt	(200)
Total purchase price	590
Less: Cash of X	(40)
Cash flow on acquisition net of cash acquired	550

B. Property, Plant and Equipment

During the period, the Group acquired property, plant and equipment with an aggregate cost of 1,250 of which 900 was acquired by means of finance leases. Cash payments of 350 were made to purchase property, plant and equipment.

C. Cash and Cash Equivalents

Cash and cash equivalents consist of cash on hand and balances with banks, and investments in money market instruments. Cash and cash equivalents included in the cash flow statement comprise the following balance sheet amounts:

	19-2	19-1
Cash on hand and balances with banks	40	25
Short-term investments	370	135
Cash and cash equivalents as previously reported	410	160
Effect of exchange rate changes	-	(40)
Cash and cash equivalents as restated	410	120

Cash and cash equivalents at the end of the period include deposits with banks of 100 held by a subsidiary which are not freely remissible to the holding company because of currency exchange restrictions.

The Group has undrawn borrowing facilities of 2,000 of which 700 may be used only for future expansion.

D. Segment Information

	Segment A	Segment B	Total
Cash flows from:			
Operating activities	1,700	(140)	1,560
Investing activities	(640)	160	(480)
Financing activities	(570)	(220)	(790)
	490	(200)	290

Alternative Presentation
(indirect method)

As an alternative, in an indirect method cash flow statement, operating profit before working capital changes is sometimes presented as follows:

Revenues excluding investment income	30,650
Operating expense excluding depreciation	(26,910)
Operating profit before working capital changes	3,740

Appendix B

Cash Flow Statement for a Financial Institution

The appendix is illustrative only and does not form part of the Standard. The purpose of the appendix is to illustrate the application of the Standard to assist in clarifying its meaning.

1. The example shows only current period amounts. Comparative amounts for the preceding period are required to be presented in accordance with IAS 1 *Presentation of Financial Statements*.

2. The example is presented using the direct method.

Cash flows from operating activities

Interest and commission receipts	28,447	
Interest payments	(23,463)	
Recoveries on loans previously written off	237	
Cash payments to employees and suppliers	(997)	
	4,224	
(Increase) decrease in operating assets:		
Short-term funds	(650)	
Deposits held for regulatory or monetary control purposes	234	
Funds advanced to customers	(288)	
Net increase in credit card receivables	(360)	
Other short-term negotiable securities	(120)	
Increase (decrease) in operating liabilities:		
Deposits from customers	600	
Negotiable certificates of deposit	(200)	
Net cash from operating activities before income tax	3,440	
Income taxes paid	(100)	
Net cash from operating activities		3,340
Cash flows from investing activities		
Disposal of subsidiary Y	50	
Dividends received	200	
Interest received	300	
Proceeds from sales of non-dealing securities	1,200	
Purchase of non-dealing securities	(600)	
Purchase of property, plant and equipment	(500)	
Net cash from investing activities		650
Cash flows from financing activities		
Issue of loan capital	1,000	
Issue of preference shares by subsidiary undertaking	800	
Repayment of long-term borrowings	(200)	
Net decrease in other borrowings	(1,000)	
Dividends paid	(400)	
Net cash from financing activities		200
Effects of exchange rate changes on cash and cash equivalents		600
Net increase in cash and cash equivalents		4,790
Cash and cash equivalents at beginning of period		4,050
Cash and cash equivalents at end of period		8,840